Strategic Energy Policy

Challenges for the 21ST Century

*Report of an Independent Task Force
Cosponsored by the
James A. Baker III Institute
for Public Policy of Rice University
and the
Council on Foreign Relations*

Edward L. Morse, Chair
Amy Myers Jaffe, Project Director

The mission of the *Baker Institute* is to help bridge the gap between the theory and practice of public policy by drawing together experts from academia, government, the media, business, and nongovernmental organizations. By involving both policymakers and scholars, the Institute seeks to improve the debate on selected public policy issues and to make a difference in the formulation, implementation, and evaluation of public policy, both domestic and international. The Baker Institute is an integral part of Rice University, one of the nation's most distinguished institutions of higher learning, located in Houston, Texas. Rice's faculty and students play an important role in its research programs and public events.

The research and views expressed in this paper are those of the Independent Task Force, and do not necessarily represent the views of the James A. Baker III Institute for Public Policy.

Founded in 1921, the *Council on Foreign Relations* is a nonpartisan membership organization, research center, and publisher. It is dedicated to increasing America's understanding of the world and contributing ideas to U.S. foreign policy. The Council accomplishes this mainly by promoting constructive discussions both in private and in public, and by publishing *Foreign Affairs*, the leading journal on global issues. The Council is host to the widest possible range of views, but an advocate of none, though its research fellows and Independent Task Forces do take policy stands.

The Council will sponsor an Independent Task Force when (1) an issue of current and critical importance to U.S. foreign policy arises, and (2) it seems that a group diverse in backgrounds and perspectives may, nonetheless, be able to reach a meaningful consensus on a policy through private and nonpartisan deliberations. Typically, a Task Force meets between two and five times over a brief period to ensure the relevance of its work.

Upon reaching a conclusion, a Task Force issues a report, and the Council publishes its text and posts it on the Council website (www.cfr.org). Task Force Reports can take three forms: (1) a strong and meaningful policy consensus, with Task Force members endorsing the general policy thrust and judgments reached by the group, though not necessarily every finding and recommendation; (2) a report stating the various policy positions, each as sharply and fairly as possible; or (3) a "Chairman's Report," where Task Force members who agree with the Chairman's Report may associate themselves with it, while those who disagree may submit dissenting statements. Upon reaching a conclusion, a Task Force may also ask individuals who were not members of the Task Force to associate themselves with the Task Force Report to enhance its impact. All Task Force Reports "benchmark" their findings against current administration policy in order to make explicit areas of agreement and disagreement. The Task Force is solely responsible for its report. The Council takes no institutional position.

For further information about the Council or this Task Force, please write the Council on Foreign Relations, 58 East 68th Street, New York, NY 10021, or call the Director of Communications at (212) 434-9400. Visit our website at www.cfr.org.

CONTENTS

FOREWORD

For many decades now, the United States has been without an energy policy. Now, the consequences of not having an energy policy that can satisfy our energy requirements on a sustainable basis have revealed themselves in California. Now, there could be more Californias in America's future. President George W. Bush and his administration need to tell these agonizing truths to the American people and thereby lay the basis for a new and viable U.S. energy policy.

That Americans face long-term energy delivery challenges and volatile energy prices is the failure of both Democrats and Republicans to fashion a workable energy policy. Energy policy was allowed to drift by both political parties despite its centrality to America's domestic economy and to our nation's security. It was permitted to drift despite the fact that virtually every American recession since the late 1940s has been preceded by spikes in oil prices. The American people need to know about this situation and be told as well that there are no easy or quick solutions to today's energy problems. The president has to begin educating the public about this reality and start building a broad base of popular support for the hard policy choices ahead.

This recommendation sits at the core of an Independent Task Force Report sponsored by our two organizations. The Task Force was chaired by Edward L. Morse, a widely recognized authority on energy, and ably assisted by Amy Myers Jaffe of the James A. Baker III Institute for Public Policy of Rice University. The Task Force included experts from every segment of the world of energy—producers, consumers, environmentalists, national security experts, and others.

There are no easy Solomonic solutions to energy crises, only hard policy tradeoffs between legitimate and competing interests. Tightening environmental regulations, among other factors, have discouraged the rapid expansion of badly needed energy infrastructure in many U.S. locations. But Americans are also demanding a cleaner environment and cleaner energy.

Strong economic growth across the globe and new global demands for more energy have meant the end of sustained surplus capacity in hydrocarbon fuels and the beginning of capacity limitations. In fact, the world is currently precariously close to utilizing all of its available oil-production capacity, raising the chances of an oil-supply crisis with more substantial consequences than seen in three decades. These limits mean that America can no longer assume that oil-producing states will provide more oil. Nor is it strategically and politically desirable to remedy our present tenuous situation by simply increasing our dependence on a few foreign sources.

So, we come to the report's central dilemma: the American people continue to demand plentiful and cheap energy without sacrifice or inconvenience. But emerging technologies are not yet commercially viable to fill shortages and will not be for some time. Nor is surplus energy capacity available at this time to meet such demands. Indeed, the situation is worse than the oil shocks of the past because in the present energy situation, the tight oil market condition is coupled with shortages of natural gas in the United States, heating fuels for the winter, and electricity supplies in certain localities.

This Independent Task Force Report outlines some of the hard choices that should be considered and recommends specific policy approaches to secure the energy future of the United States. These choices will affect other U.S. policy objectives: U.S. policy toward the Middle East; U.S. policy toward Russia and the former Soviet Union states and China; the fight against international terrorism; and environmental and international trade policy, including our position on the European Union (EU) energy charter, economic sanctions, North American Free Trade Agreement (NAFTA), and foreign trade credits and aid. The Bush administration is in a unique position to articulate these tradeoffs in a nonpartisan manner and to rally the support of the American public. U.S. strategic energy policy must prioritize and coordinate domestic and foreign policy choices and objectives, where possible.

Moreover, the energy problem is inexorably intertwined with the fundamental challenge of creating sustainable economic growth without sacrificing environmental protection. The pursuit of a solution demands a major national effort.

Finally, we come to the pleasant task of thanking those on the Independent Task Force who were instrumental in supporting Ed Morse and Amy Jaffe in the organization of the Task Force's meetings and the preparation of the report. We would like to thank Colonel James E. Sikes Jr., of the U.S. Army, who served as a military fellow at the Council on Foreign Relations this year and also was the project coordinator of the Task Force; Sarah Saghir, a research associate at the Council on Foreign Relations; W. O. King Jr., Baker Institute administrator; and Jason Lyons, Baker Institute Energy Forum staff assistant. And for them and us, special thanks to all the participating members of the Task Force for their expertise, ideas, stimulating debate, and hard work.

Edward Djerejian
Director
Baker Institute

Leslie H. Gelb
President
Council on Foreign Relations

ACKNOWLEDGMENTS

The Independent Task Force on Strategic Energy Policy Challenges for the 21st Century was a collective endeavor reflecting the contributions and hard work of many individuals. First and foremost, I am indebted to the superb chair, Dr. Edward L. Morse, for his dedication, wisdom, insights, superior writing and editing skills, guidance, and steadfast support during the past five months. Ed Morse made this challenging assignment look easy through his outstanding leadership and deep analytic understanding of the subject matter. I congratulate him on drawing together this outstanding group of professionals and policymakers into a broad consensus on highly complex and divisive issues. But most importantly, I would like to thank Ed Morse for his loyalty and faith in me that extends back more than a decade and has truly made a difference in my life and career.

I am also indebted to the Task Force members, observers, and reviewers who generously shared experience, information, ideas, and concepts. Their energetic participation in three complicated video conferences and teleconferences from diverse locations and time zones offered invaluable insight, suggestions, and advice during December, January, and February 2000–01. This report reflects their views and concurrence on the broad thrusts of this examination of U.S. energy policy. Although not every member signed on to every word or prescription, I am grateful for every view presented in this report, including the concurrence with the main report as well as additional views and dissent. The dedication of our Task Force members to enhancing the debate on this important matter of public policy is the cornerstone to a better framework.

The Task Force benefited greatly from the counsel and input provided by a group of reviewers with broad academic, economic, and energy expertise. These individuals reviewed drafts of the report at various stages and participated in the Task Force meetings. Throughout the period of their supportive collaboration, the

Task Force benefited from their keen observations, and their insights greatly enhanced the final report. Additionally, the Task Force recognizes the contributions of those members of the James A. Baker III Institute for Public Policy and the Council on Foreign Relations staff acting as observers for the Task Force.

I want to thank Sarah Miller, vice president of the Energy Intelligence Group, for her invaluable editing contribution to this project. Also, I extend my deep gratitude to the staff that made this project run so well, including Colonel James E. Sikes Jr., U.S. Army, the project coordinator and military fellow for 2000–01 who worked closely with me; Sarah Saghir, research associate of the Council on Foreign Relations; and my invaluable partner, Jason Lyons, the Baker Institute Energy Forum program assistant without whom it would not have been possible to complete this project in a timely fashion. Other staff members of the Baker Institute and Council on Foreign Relations also provided invaluable support, including the technical adviser at the Council, Irina Faskianos, who is the National Program deputy director; W.O. King Jr., Baker Institute administrator; Jay Guerrero, Baker Institute events coordinator; Calvin Avery, technical adviser; and other Baker Institute technical staff, Katie Hamilton and Suzanne Stroud. I would also like to thank my research interns Matthew Chen and Rachel Krause. I extend a special thanks to Falah Aljibury for his astute observations about the Middle East and his always sympathetic ear. Finally, and most importantly, to my husband and three great children, Jordan, Rebecca, and Daniel, for the personal sacrifices made in the hopes of a better U.S. energy policy and safer environment.

The Task Force was made possible through the generous support of Khalid Al-Turki, a member of the Council's International Advisory Board. We are also grateful for the Arthur Ross Foundation's support for Task Forces.

The Task Force reflected a productive institutional collaboration between the James A. Baker III Institute for Public Policy and the Council on Foreign Relations. I want to express my special appreciation to Ambassador Edward Djerejian, director of the Baker Institute, for his mentoring, wise guidance, and insights, and to

Acknowledgements

Dr. Ric Stoll, associate director for academic affairs at the Baker Institute, whose astute advice and counsel has kept me on track for this and many other equally challenging projects. I also owe a debt of gratitude to the faculty of Rice University who have taken me in and taught me the art form of academic discourse, and to Joe Barnes and Robert Manning for their excellent counsel in matters of policy formation and writing. At the Council in New York, I am grateful to Leslie H. Gelb, the Council's president, for his support and astute comments that helped us develop a clear and effective draft; Mike Peters, senior vice president, for his general assistance in resourcing the Task Force; Director of Publishing Patricia Dorff; and Communications Director April Palmerlee.

This final report reflects an extraordinary amount of work by a broad range of experts who took the time to participate in this important endeavor. They responded in detail to several drafts, improving the structure, providing understanding on regional issues, providing information on federal and state regulatory policies, expanding the horizon of the members on the impact of globalization on energy issues, and filling in the gaps while suggesting new approaches to challenging problems. Without the hard work and collaboration of the Task Force members this project would not have been possible.

Amy Myers Jaffe
Project Director

EXECUTIVE SUMMARY

THE CHALLENGE

For many decades the United States has not had a comprehensive energy policy. Now, the consequences of this complacency have revealed themselves in California. Now, there could be more California-like situations in America's future. President George W. Bush and his administration need to tell these agonizing truths to the American people and lay the basis for a comprehensive, long-term U.S. energy security policy.

That Americans face long-term situations such as frequent sporadic shortages of energy, energy price volatility, and higher energy prices is not the fault of President Bush. The failure to fashion a workable energy policy rests at the feet of both Democrats and Republicans. Both major political parties allowed energy policy to drift despite its centrality to America's domestic economy and to national security. Energy policy was permitted to drift even though oil price spikes preceded virtually every American recession since the late 1940s. The American people must know about this situation and be told as well that there are no easy or quick solutions to today's energy problems. The president has to begin educating the public about this reality and start building a broad base of popular support for the hard policy choices ahead.

This executive summary and the full report address the following questions. What are the potential effects of the critical energy situation for the United States? How did this critical energy situation arise? What are the U.S. policy options to deal with the energy situation? What should the United States do now?

WHAT ARE THE POTENTIAL EFFECTS OF THE CRITICAL ENERGY SITUATION FOR THE UNITED STATES?

As the 21st century opens, the energy sector is in critical condition. A crisis could erupt at any time from any number of factors and would inevitably affect every country in today's globalized world. While the origins of a crisis are hard to pinpoint, it is clear that energy disruptions could have a potentially enormous impact on the U.S. and the world economy, and would affect U.S. national security and foreign policy in dramatic ways.

An accident on the Alaska pipeline that brings the bulk of North Slope crude oil to market would have the same impact as a revolution cutting off supplies from a major Middle East oil producer. An attack on the California electric power grid could cripple that state's economy for years, affecting all of the economies of the Pacific Basin. A revolution in Indonesia would paralyze the liquefied natural gas (LNG) import-dependent economies of South Korea and Japan, affecting domestic politics and all of their trading partners. While oil is still readily available on international markets, prices have doubled from the levels that helped spur rapid economic growth through much of the 1990s. And with spare capacity scarce and Middle East tensions high, chances are greater than at any point in the last two decades of an oil supply disruption that would even more severely test the nation's security and prosperity. The situation is, by analogy, like traveling in a car with broken shock absorbers at very high speeds such as ninety miles an hour. As long as the paving on the highway is perfectly smooth, no injury to the driver will result from the poor decision of not spending the money to fix the car. But if the car confronts a large bump or pothole, the injury to the driver could be quite severe regardless of whether he or she was wearing a seatbelt.

An energy crisis need not arise abruptly. One can emerge through slower contagions. Electricity outages already have our most populous state in a vice and are threatening to spread from California to other parts of the country. Natural gas is available to heat homes and run power plants in some parts of the United States only because prices soared over the winter to many times previous historic peaks. Gas markets dealt successfully with a supply shortage, but only at the cost of driving a few lower priority industrial users to close plants and lay off workers, and many to desert gas for fuels that were more polluting. If economic growth continues, price spikes and supply shortages could become widespread recurring events challenging expectations of free energy and making the United States appear more similar to a poor developing country.

HOW DID THIS CRITICAL ENERGY SITUATION ARISE?

How the United States and indeed the rest of the world got into this difficulty is a long and complicated story. The situation did not develop overnight. But one of the fundamental reasons it could develop is unambiguous. The United States has not had a comprehensive, integrated strategic energy policy for decades. Instead, many factors were allowed to converge to contribute to today's critical energy situation. Infrastructure constraints, inadequate infrastructure development, rapid global economic expansion, the lack of spare capacity and the changes in inventory dynamics, a lack of trained energy sector workers, and the unintended side effects of energy market deregulation and market liberalization all contributed to the critical energy situation.

The reasons for the energy challenge have nothing to do with the global hydrocarbon resource base, which is still enormous, and everything to do with infrastructure constraints that can and must be addressed as a matter of the highest priority at the highest level of government. In the United States, years of rapid economic expansion coincided with tightening restrictions on building new facilities and capital flight from smokestack to high-tech industries that discouraged investment in conventional energy sources. The result was sudden, severe strains at critical links in the energy supply chain. Now, acute shortages are evident in electric power generation and transmission capacity. Natural gas production was not adequate last year to replenish inventories during low demand seasons, leading to this year's soaring prices. Oil refineries are barely able to produce enough of the cleaner fuels that are increasingly in demand, refined product imports are soaring, and isolated but politically troublesome shortages have already occurred in both gas and heating oil. Oil and gas pipelines are operating at so close to capacity that unexpected outages can quickly lead to price spikes and even regional physical shortages, as witnessed with heating oil in parts of New England last winter. And the industry faces critical shortages of trained personnel, as well as of the capital equipment required to overcome these constraints. At the same time, to bolster profitability and share prices, industry has adopted strict "just-in-time inventory" policies that further weaken the safety net.

Internationally, too, rapid economic growth during the past decade has stretched to the limit world capacity to produce oil and natural gas. Falling real prices for oil over much of the last two decades gave the few producing nations with the bulk of the world's reserves little incentive to invest in new infrastructure as the capacity cushion left from the 1970s gradually disappeared. Meanwhile, across much of the developing world, energy infrastructure is being severely tested by the expanding material demands of a growing middle class, especially in the high-growth, high-population economies of Asia. As demand growth collided with supply and capacity limits at the end of the last century, prices rose across the energy spectrum, at home and abroad.

Since the 1970s, governments around the globe have, to varying degrees, retreated from heavy regulation of national energy sectors. Market forces were freed to stimulate investment and allocate resources. And up to a point, the strategy worked. In the United States, as elsewhere, deregulation did initially bring the expected lower energy prices in most cases. But market liberalization brought some less desirable consequences, as well. For all their advantages, deregulation and reliance on consumer preferences failed to provide incentives either to build surplus infrastructure capacity or hold the inventories of fuel needed to smooth out market dislocations. Capacity cushions that had built up earlier gradually eroded. Shortages that have been years in the making seem to be springing up overnight. As a result, today's situation arose by stealth, as years of rapid growth crashed into the physical supply barricades that were erected by decades of underinvestment in energy infrastructure.

WHAT ARE THE U.S. POLICY OPTIONS TO DEAL WITH THE ENERGY SITUATION?

There are no easy overnight solutions. The United States faces three policy paths to deal with the energy problem. One option is to continue the easy approach of "muddling through" with marginal Strategic Petroleum Reserve (SPR) management and complete free market solutions. A second option is to take a near-term, narrow approach by expanding supply to ensure cheap energy while enduring conflict with environmental and consumer groups and others. Finally, the United States could develop a comprehensive and balanced energy security policy with near-term actions and long-term initiatives addressing both the supply side and demand side including diversification of energy supply resources, which would enable the United States to escape from a pattern of recurring energy crises.

The nation, like the international economy on which it depends for prosperity, confronts a deep-seated energy problem that demands attention at the highest level of government and industry, if it is not to act as a clamp on sustained and sustainable economic growth—in the United States and across the world. Long-term, dedicated programs are required and explicit trade-offs might well be needed between energy objectives and other areas of public concern, including economic growth, the state of the human habitat, and certain foreign policy objectives, if these problems are to be overcome. Long-term problems require long-term solutions and may literally require a higher price of energy goods if the right supply and demand responses are to emerge.

Supply-side responses alone will not suffice. To be effective and politically acceptable, solutions must also focus on demand-side efficiency and must address the environmental and foreign policy concerns that frame so much of the American public's attitude toward energy development and use. Indeed, if quick fixes on the supply side alone brought prices back down in the absence of effective efforts to promote energy efficiency, they might actually prolong the problem the United States now faces in the energy arena, by bringing even greater reliance on imports.

As it is, national solutions alone cannot work. Politicians still speak of U.S. energy independence, while the United States is importing more than half of its oil supplies and may soon for the first time become reliant on sources outside North America for substantial amounts of natural gas. More flexible environmental regulation and opening of more federal lands to drilling might slow but cannot stop this process. Dependence is so incredibly large, and growing so inexorably, that national autonomy is simply not a viable goal. In the global economy, it may not even be a desirable one.

WHAT SHOULD THE UNITED STATES DO NOW?

The United States must stake out new paths as it adjusts to economic interdependence in energy. Alliances, effective diplomacy, freer trade, and innovative multilateral trade and investment frameworks will all be tools for securing reliable energy supplies in the 21st century. Traditional policies and long-standing institutional approaches, developed mainly in the 1970s, are inadequate to the challenge. Much has changed in the last thirty years, yet institutions such as the International Energy Agency (IEA) have done little to revamp their outmoded missions, memberships, and mechanisms.

The energy problems we face today are complex, and our response to them must range from a review of our domestic environmental, tax, and regulatory structures to a reassessment of the role of energy in American foreign policy. This uncomfortable truth is largely absent in today's public debate, which is all too often marked by simplistic analysis and debilitating accusation. We need not to apportion blame but to seek workable, integrated solutions that balance energy priorities with economic, environmental, and national security objectives.

Such a strategy will require difficult tradeoffs, in both domestic and foreign policy. But there is no alternative. And there is no time to waste. The problems facing the energy sector will take at least three to five years to solve. Some will take longer. Short-term measures can alleviate immediate bottlenecks or buttress emergency preparedness, but it takes years to license and build power plants, lay new pipelines, expand refineries, train skilled workers and engineers, and develop new oil and gas fields—much less negotiate new international agreements and understandings. A successful U.S. energy policy must encompass not only quick fixes, but also long-term initiatives that produce results well into the future.

Until the emerging constraints are overcome, government will need to increase its vigilance and be prepared to deal with sudden supply disruptions. The consequences of inaction could be grave. Not only is economic growth at risk. But high prices and sporadic dislocations threaten public acceptance of market solutions and foster support for a return to regulation. The government will need to work hard to ward off political pressures, both at home and abroad, that could undermine the huge gains that have been made and to assure that markets become more efficient. Disadvantaged segments of the population need to be convinced that the right course of action is not a new form of government regulation.

Delay will simply raise the costs. As each year passes, the investment required to overcome supply bottlenecks grows. The president needs to act now to reassess the nation's long-term objectives in this most important area of policy, with an eye to developing a comprehensive approach that can assure economic prosperity and international security for future generations.

INTRODUCTION AND BACKGROUND

Recent energy price spikes, electricity outages in California, localized oil product and natural gas shortages, and extreme energy price volatility have ushered in a new era of energy scarcity. The process of managing and working off surplus capacities that marked the past two decades is complete. Supply constraints have emerged across the energy spectrum, not only in the United States but around the world, presenting fundamental obstacles to continued economic growth and prosperity. The challenge of the new era is marshaling capital to develop adequate resources and infrastructure to meet rising demand for energy, in a manner that is consistent with environmental goals.

The cause of these energy infrastructure constraints is evident: persistent underinvestment juxtaposed with strong economic and oil-demand growth. Their solution will require a complex set of well-coordinated domestic and international efforts. The fact that oil's input into gross domestic product (GDP) has been nearly cut in half during the last fifty years does not mean that output can expand with no increase in energy. Nor does it break the link evident in the fact that virtually every U.S. recession since the late 1940s has been preceded by a sharp rise in the price of oil. (See Appendix A.) The economic reversal now looming will, if it develops into a full-fledged recession, be no exception.

The United States faces a steep decline rate in its domestic oil fields and, to some extent, in its natural gas fields. Proven oil reserves have declined from about 26 billion barrels in 1990 to 20 billion today. Proven gas reserves had slipped to 164 trillion cubic feet in January 2000, from 177.6 trillion cubic feet a decade ago. However, this does not mean that ultimate resource levels were a major factor in the tightening of U.S. energy markets. The United States managed to produce 20 billion barrels during the decade in which the proven reserve levels slipped by 6 billion barrels, and it still has more proven oil in the lower forty-eight states today than it did in 1930, indicating a still substantial replacement rate. Even more important for the future, estimates of the amount of undiscovered oil outside the United States are still rising, according to the U.S. Geological Survey, while the global search for natural gas has barely begun. The world will not run short of hydrocarbons in the foreseeable future.

The problem is one of developing these and other fuels and getting them to the consumers who need them. U.S. investment aimed at accomplishing this failed to keep pace with rising demand in part because energy industry profits were dismal through much of the 1990s, hitting bottom during the oil price collapse at the decade's end. The situation was exacerbated because low returns coincided with tightening environmental restrictions and an uneven regulatory process, especially in the electricity sector. No new oil refineries are likely to be built in the United States, given the high costs of environmental compliance and historically low returns on investment. Meanwhile, U.S. product imports shot up by nearly 20 percent last year from 1999, to 2.25 million barrels a day, and appear to be growing even more rapidly this year.

Chronically low prices, adverse fiscal regulations, interstate disputes about pipeline rights of way, and restrictions on land access have all undermined growth in natural gas availability—at the same time that its clean burn has encouraged wider use of gas to heat buildings and fuel power plants and industry. In both 1998 and 1999, investment hit bottom amid plunging oil prices, and extremely mild winter weather masked both the rapid growth in underlying demand for natural gas and the erosion of spare "deliverability." All these events prevented the run-up in prices that might have sparked investment earlier. Then, in 2000 and early 2001, extreme weather—a hot summer and a cold start to the winter—suddenly inflated the previously hidden underlying growth in gas demand. Lags in the supply system prevented a rapid response, leading to record low inventories and soaring prices. Some relief may now be on the way, given rising rig counts and increased imports from Canada, accompanied by fuel switching and closure of uneconomic industrial capacity. Yet questions remain as to how robust the domestic supply response will be, given high depletion rates in North America and a shortage of rigs and trained personnel.

The story in the power sector is similar. No new nuclear plants have been ordered in the United States in more than twenty years. For the last decade, well over 90 percent of all new power plants ordered have been gas-fired. In some states, such as California, environmental concerns raised the bar to impractical levels even for construction of conventionally fueled electric power stations. High gas prices, an unusually cold winter, an explosion at a major natural gas pipeline last August, maintenance closures at nuclear power plants, and a drop in hydroelectric power converged with incomplete deregulation to produce devastating shortages in the California power grid. The resulting public outcry has called into question the benefits of electricity deregulation, despite relatively successful programs in other parts of the United States. Spare generation capacity also looks to be in short supply in the New York State region, where brownouts could emerge in the summer of 2001 if hot temperatures inflate demand for air conditioning.

Other parts of the U.S. energy infrastructure are afflicted as well. Permits and rights of way are nearly impossible to obtain for new pipelines, especially oil lines, and tanker shortages threaten to occur again partly because of environmental regulations.

The 1998–99 downturn in U.S. oil and gas investment came against the backdrop of years of reduced oil-field development spending by state-owned oil companies in Organization of Petroleum Exporting Countries (OPEC) members. Internal political pressures impelled governments as diverse as those of Saudi Arabia and Venezuela to dedicate more of their oil revenue to social programs. This converged with an unexpectedly robust world economy in the late 1990s to virtually wipe out excess capacity. That, in turn, sparked anew debates about the depletion of conventional hydrocarbons in a way that sometimes obscured the true nature of the problem.

The enormous swings in energy prices over the last four years have affected different parts of the world differently. But they have been good for no one. In 1998, most of the world benefited as stunningly low crude oil prices filtered through consuming economies. Yet a handful of oil exporting countries faced a fall of up to 50 percent in their national incomes within a year—an experience that had severe political and economic repercussions. Governments changed in Algeria, Brunei, Indonesia, Nigeria, and Venezuela, as loss of income exacerbated other difficulties. The price collapse threatened to destabilize societies as diverse as Russia and Indonesia. The following year, non-OPEC producers Mexico, Norway, and Oman joined with OPEC to remedy the situation by cutting production, thus pushing the burden back onto the rest of the world— but not before resentment had built up against the industrialized nations for turning a blind eye when prices fell so low. Industrialized countries, developing-country energy importers, and energy exporting countries have common concerns about severe price volatility and its impact on the domestic and international "political economy." The challenge now is how to turn this common perception into effective joint action.

In the past, energy crises have appeared simply to fade away over time. Sometimes, as in the late 1970s and early 1980s, recession solved the problem by radically reducing global energy demand. At other times, technological improvements reduced costs and created new efficiencies on both the supply and demand sides, fostering complacency among policymakers. Government attention to energy issues has tended to fade as prices fall. That complacency could be justified so long as surplus capacities existed. But in a world of energy capacity constraint, complacency could shackle the U.S. economy for years to come. If it does not respond strategically to the current energy circumstances, the United States risks perpetuating the unacceptable leverage of adversaries and leaving its economy vulnerable to volatile energy prices.

The time has come for a fresh strategic assessment of U.S. energy policy—one that intelligently balances potentially conflicting objectives of energy supply promotion, sustainable economic growth, environmental protection, and national security. A comprehensive effort is required that will integrate energy with other policy goals, while developing new sources of supply and finding ways to prune expected demand growth in order to assure that clean and adequate energy supplies will be available. This Task Force offers

Strategic Energy Policy

a unique perspective on the problems at hand and the difficult choices that will be required to deal with them effectively.

THE PAST TWO DECADES: A REVIEW OF POLICY

Through the 1980s and 1990s, the centerpiece of U.S. energy policy was to foster, at home and abroad, deregulated markets that efficiently allocated capital, provided a maximum of consumer choice, and fostered low prices through competition. U.S. policy also favored diversity of supply, both geographically and in terms of energy sources. Domestically, infrastructure needs have been left to market forces. This hands-off policy has generally led to lower real energy costs. But this, in turn, has brought a dramatic slowdown in efficiency gains and a potentially dangerous complacency about energy supplies, energy efficiency, demand management, and conservation.

Tax policy was not utilized—as it was in Europe and Japan—to discourage use of hydrocarbons or to promote environmentally friendly fuels. Transportation's share of petroleum use had risen to 66 percent by 1995 from 52 percent in 1970, and could hit 70 percent by 2010 if new technologies are not put in place. Improvements in automobile mileage standards could dramatically influence these growth rates in U.S. consumption, while keeping the automotive industry competitive.

At the same time as it was ignoring demand management, U.S. policy frequently allowed energy supply goals to take a back seat to environmental considerations when it came to land management, emissions, and other policy requirements. Even in foreign policy, where the United States has frequently stated its desire to see new acreage opened to oil and gas exploration, it has not backed up its words with active support of these goals. On the contrary, it has frequently used energy sanctions as an instrument of foreign policy, blocking targeted countries from trade or investment, while making energy goals secondary to other foreign policy objectives.

For the most part, U.S. international oil policy has relied on maintenance of free access to Middle East Gulf oil and free access for Gulf exports to world markets. The United States has forged a special relationship with certain key Middle East exporters, which had an expressed interest in stable oil prices and, we assumed, would adjust their oil output to keep prices at levels that would neither discourage global economic growth nor fuel inflation. Taking this dependence a step further, the U.S. government has operated under the assumption that the national oil companies of these countries would make the investments needed to maintain enough surplus capacity to form a cushion against disruptions elsewhere. For several years, these assumptions appeared justified.

But recently, things have changed. These Gulf allies are finding their domestic and foreign policy interests increasingly at odds with U.S. strategic considerations, especially as Arab-Israeli tensions flare. They have become less inclined to lower oil prices in exchange for security of markets, and evidence suggests that investment is not being made in a timely enough manner to increase production capacity in line with growing global needs. A trend toward anti-Americanism could affect regional leaders' ability to cooperate with the United States in the energy area.

The resulting tight markets have increased U.S. and global vulnerability to disruption and provided adversaries undue potential influence over the price of oil. Iraq has become a key "swing" producer, posing a difficult situation for the U.S. government.

Another new element is adding to vulnerability. Deregulation has encouraged U.S. and other energy companies to focus more single-mindedly on maximizing their competitive positions. One tool has been to slash inventories—cushions that are expensive but are needed to smooth out the functioning of markets during temporary dislocations.

HOW DID ENERGY MARKETS SUDDENLY BECOME SO
CONSTRAINED?

By the end of the 1970s, a consensus had emerged that the world economy had entered a "permanent" period of tightness in energy supplies. But actually, the high prices that followed the 1973 and 1979 oil crises attracted increased investment in energy resources and energy efficiency. Oil use dropped initially in absolute terms, especially in the power sector, where robust growth of nuclear power and increased reliance on coal replaced it. At the same time, the oil shocks and other factors contributed to a slowdown in some major industrialized economies, further reinforcing the substantial drop in oil use. Higher prices also encouraged investment in conventional and nonconventional fuels, especially outside of OPEC, as well as in energy efficiency. As a result, for most of the late 1980s and early 1990s, real oil and natural gas prices returned to historically "normal" and more moderate levels.

New sources of oil supply outside of OPEC countries contributed to this price slide, as did increases in production from Iraq and Iran, whose capacities had earlier been constrained by war. Resource nationalism began to ebb, as deregulation and liberalization of markets seemed to provide energy consumers near-unlimited resources at low prices, whether in the form of oil, electricity, or natural gas. Surplus capacities along the entire energy chain—accumulated in the days of government-subsidized industry and falling demand—meant that there could be an expansion of energy use without significantly affecting underlying costs. These surpluses were found in all aspects of the energy industry, including refineries, tankers and pipelines, offshore and land rigs, other oil-field equipment, and power-generating capacity.

Concern about the adverse environmental impacts of higher energy use prompted public authorities throughout the industrial world to tighten regulations. These measures could be implemented without fear of price consequences because energy supplies were ample. New technologies were expected to continue reducing the costs of energy production, while at the same time creating adequate supplies to meet demand. Market deregulation and the emergence of futures markets reinforced the view that energy supplies would always be ample, while giving energy producers new financial instruments with which to mitigate price risks.

The persistence of surplus capacities also allowed policymakers to place a greater emphasis on non-energy goals than on timely resource development, without fear of economic consequences. Environmental restrictions on oil products were tightened, elaborate permit procedures for new infrastructure were created, and importantly, economic sanctions were imposed on key oil-producing countries for an array of foreign policy reasons. The U.S. government even moved 180 degrees away from its policy of the 1970s and began to adopt secondary boycotts of certain oil-producing countries in an effort to combat terrorism. Sanctions policy was buttressed by the belief in many U.S. circles that economic warfare was partially responsible for the collapse of the Soviet Union.

The August 1990 Iraqi invasion of Kuwait witnessed a major test of global energy security. That test was readily met, creating a deeper sense of complacency among oil-consuming nations. With the end of the Cold War, U.S. leadership was able to forge an international coalition to repel Iraq. Although oil-supply security was a major issue cementing the coalition, it could be assigned a back seat to issues of international order because of three critical factors:

1. **Surplus Capacity:** The U.N. embargo on Iraqi and Kuwaiti oil was made possible by the existence of extensive surplus production capacity elsewhere. In August, some 5 million barrels a day of production was taken off the market through the embargo. By December, all of the lost production was made up through increases from Saudi Arabia, Venezuela, Abu Dhabi, and other OPEC nations, which had been carrying vast spare capacity and were willing to assist the coalition against Iraq. Previous surpluses also had cushioned the market with unusually high commercial stocks of crude oil and products.

2. **Strategic Reserves:** The more than 1 billion barrels of strategic petroleum reserves in International Energy Agency (IEA)-member countries loomed over the market, depriving OPEC or other oil producers of market power. It also restrained speculators, who would lose financially if those reserves were released. In the case of the Gulf War, the IEA system fulfilled its original mission to serve as a deterrent to mar-

ket manipulation by adversaries during a crisis. Its very existence served to damp prices under the new market conditions.

3. **Market Mechanisms:** The deregulation of petroleum and refined product markets in the 1980s and the growth of futures and forward markets provided rapid and effective adjustment mechanisms. These developments facilitated refiners' orderly transition from Kuwaiti and Iraqi supplies to replacement oil from Saudi Arabia, Venezuela, and Abu Dhabi, whether those refiners were in East Asia, Europe, or the Western Hemisphere.

What Has Changed?

Perhaps the most significant difference between now and a decade ago is the extraordinarily rapid erosion of spare capacities at critical segments of energy chains. Today, shortfalls appear to be endemic. Among the most extraordinary of these losses in spare capacity is in the oil arena. In 1985, when oil prices collapsed, OPEC was estimated to have some 15 million barrels a day (b/d) of shut-in production capacity, equal to perhaps 50 percent of its theoretical capacity (Iran and Iraq were at war with one another at the time) and 25 percent of global demand. By 1990, when Iraq invaded Kuwait, spare capacity globally was still about 5 to 5.5 million barrels per day, which was the amount of oil taken off the market by the U.N. embargo. That was about 20 percent of OPEC's capacity at the time and about 8 percent of global demand. This winter, before OPEC's seasonal cuts, spare capacity was a negligible 2 percent of global demand.

The surge in energy demand worldwide that combined with underinvestment to create these shortfalls has been stunning, especially in high-growth Asian economies. In the United States, oil demand has risen on average 1–2 percent per year since the late 1980s. In recent years, the rate has picked up to at least 2 percent, reflecting not only strong economic performance but also the relative neglect of policies related to conservation and energy efficiency. U.S. energy efficiency as measured by the amount of energy used per constant dollar of gross national product (GNP) declined from 8,300 British thermal units (BTUs) per 1996 U.S.

dollar thirty years ago to 4,600 BTUs in 1995. But it dropped only an additional 400 BTUs between 1995 and 1999, despite great technological advances in many sectors of the economy. The decline in petroleum used, measured in terms of thousands of BTUs per dollar of GDP, was even more radical in the twenty-five years to 1995, from $15.15 to $8.43, reflecting structural shifts in the economy and improvements in energy efficiency. However, as energy costs fell starting in the mid-1980s, promotion of energy efficiency slowed dramatically.

Although appliances have become increasingly energy-efficient, energy consumption patterns have loosened up. Nowhere is this more apparent than in the U.S. automobile sector, with the growth in demand for light trucks (pickups, sport utility vehicles [SUVs], and minivans) that burn more gasoline than smaller vehicles. The transportation sector accounts for an increasing share of petroleum use in the United States, rising from 52 percent in 1970 to 66 percent in 1995. This is expected to increase to 70 percent by 2010 unless new technologies are put in place. The United States is not unique in displaying this trend. Assuming no major breakthroughs in automotive technology, the IEA projects that 59 percent of the 41 million b/d increase in worldwide oil demand expected from 1995 to 2020 will come from the transport sector.

Efficiency has increased in the transportation sector, where average miles per gallon (mpg) for standard automobiles have increased from 15.1 in 1983 to about 21.5 in 1999. However, the potential to do much more is an attainable option. The average fuel economy of light trucks on the road is only 17.4 mpg. Ford and General Motors have vowed to improve fuel economy for certain SUVs by 25 percent by 2005, but across-the-board implementation of higher mileage standards for light trucks could substantially lower oil use in the United States.

SUVs account for 25 percent of the category of light trucks, up from 13.2 percent of all light trucks in 1992, yielding an average annual growth rate of 14 percent. The average annual growth rate for the entire light truck category was 4.42 percent. If fuel efficiency of light trucks matched that of cars, U.S. fuel savings would equal about 910,000 b/d of crude oil. If the fuel efficiency of only SUVs matched that of cars, the fuel savings would be 225,000 b/d. That is just one example of the result from disregarding demand measures, where demand management could well be the most efficient way to "develop" more oil supply in the United States.

By 2010, without government intervention, high-mileage "post-combustion" automobiles such as the gas-electric and fuel-cell hybrids could make up as much as 15–20 percent of new vehicles but would still only trim U.S. crude oil demand by 600,000 b/d, according to private studies. However, in the period between 2010–20, such technology could begin to make a significant contribution to curbing the growth in energy use. Several major car companies have announced plans to introduce new prototype hybrid cars by 2003–04.

Since 1973, the share of oil in the U.S. energy mix fell from 49.5 percent to 41 percent in 1999. But this trend could slow in the coming years if rising natural gas prices discourage gas substitution for oil. Already, fuel switching back to oil has resulted in a 500,000 to 600,000 b/d increase in oil use in the United States in early 2001, according to Department of Energy statistics.

The share of natural gas rose from 18.2 percent in 1973 to 24 percent in 1999. Nuclear power is an indigenous source of energy, unique in having the capacity to provide enough energy to last hundreds of years without emitting greenhouse gases. Nuclear energy represents 22.9 percent of total U.S. electricity generation and is expected to fall as older plants are retired and as new construction is thwarted by social concerns and by regulatory issues as well as waste-disposal obstacles. No new plants have been constructed in the United States for two decades, and if the licenses of existing plants are not granted extensions, license expiration could lead to a 50 percent reduction in nuclear generation capacity by 2020. The United States's choice of an open fuel cycle (i.e., once-through utilization of nuclear fuel followed by geological disposal) is plagued by spent-fuel isolation issues. The alternative closed fuel cycle advanced in France, Japan, and other countries (i.e., reprocessing of spent fuel to extract and recycle plutonium) is plagued by large accumulations of separated plutonium and unfavorable economics. The proliferation danger posed by separated plutonium led to a U.S. decision in the late 1970s to pursue the open fuel cycle.

Also in the 1970s and early 1980s, companies began investing in renewable technologies, but as oil prices began to fall in the mid-1980s and some investors in renewable projects failed to turn a profit, this trend also slowed. Renewable energy sources, including biomass, solar, wind, and hydro, now represent less than 10 percent of total U.S. energy use. Technological advances that have led to cost reductions in some fuels such as solar and wind represent an area for expanded attention. But hydro is the dominant renewable resource and has minimal expansion potential in the United States.

Environmental factors have also led to a decrease in the share of coal in the U.S. energy mix from 30 percent in 1973 to 23 percent currently, despite the fact that the United States has among the largest coal deposits in the world. Still, more than 50 percent of all electricity generated in the United States is fueled by coal. Internationally, coal use is expected to double in the next fifteen years. Despite governmental and industry efforts to foster clean coal technologies, coal's high carbon base has made it a subject of attack by environmental concerns. But progress has been made and can continue to be made in reducing coal emissions.

Influence of Environmental Restrictions
Besides influencing the mix of fuels used in the United States, environmental factors have also created market inefficiencies that have exacerbated the underlying tightening of energy infrastructure. Federal and state environmental regulations have created at various times anomalies in local and regional supplies. Refiners and distributors have lost much of the flexibility they used to have to move gasoline supplies around the country to keep local and regional supply in balance. Thirty years ago, U.S. refineries made gasoline, diesel, and heating oil to national standards. In recent years, petroleum companies have been required under environmental restrictions to formulate at least seven different varieties of cleaner burning fuels for national or wide-scale distribution. Nationwide, the U.S. market uses more than fifty different types of motor gasoline, comprising different regional and local environ-

mental requirements, octane levels, and seasonal fuel requirements. This "market Balkanization," as labeled by the Petroleum Industry Research Foundation, Inc., (PIRINC) has distorted markets, creating artificial supply problems as well as artificial barriers to free trade in products. The result is that local, pocketed markets with their own individual quality requirements have become extremely vulnerable to disruption and localized price spikes, raising the costs to consumers of meeting environmental goals.

The problem of Balkanization is easy to describe at a theoretical level. Uncoordinated state regulations require refiners to manufacture an increasingly large number of types of specific products and to distribute and store these products in or close to final end-user markets in the states that mandate particular specifications that differ from one another and from general norms. With the refinery system of the United States—indeed of all of the Organization for Economic Cooperation and Development (OECD) countries—constrained in terms of its ability to meet both new national and multinational specifications mandated by environmental authorities, the addition of particular state specifications stretches the physical refining and distribution system beyond its limits. The result is supply shortage and high price volatility affecting consumers in specific locations. The shortages that emerged two years ago appear inevitably bound to worsen in the decade ahead.

Boutique fuels problems have become especially acute in the gasoline and, to some extent, the distillate markets, which have become highly segmented. For gasoline, problems in the Middle West and California in 2000 are likely to be repeated this year and indefinitely into the future unless efforts are made to smooth out market segmentation. Last year, California and the Chicago markets became extremely sensitive to disruptions in local supplies. In 2000, as PIRINC has shown, a 2–3 percent—i.e., very small—supply shortfall in the Middle West region of the United States helped create sharp increases in prices of reformulated gasoline in the region. As a result, average prices there, as has recently been the case in California, rose by up to 50 cents a gallon versus better-supplied markets (e.g., the U.S. Gulf Coast region).

Introduction and Background

The distillate situation last year in the Northeast United States displayed similar bottlenecks. Differentials between New England and U.S. Gulf Coast distillate prices widened significantly—more than 12 cents a gallon both in December and January. The differentials reflected differences in inventories being held in the regions. The newly created Northeast Heating Oil Reserve partially helped to solve the problem. But it took much longer than it might have to reduce these market differentials largely because heating oil marketers were forced to use U.S.-flagged tankers to move distillate from the U.S. Gulf Coast to New England. Meanwhile, distillate was being exported from the Gulf Coast to Latin America and Europe, where price differentials were high enough to make such trade profitable.

U.S. Northeast and Atlantic Coast markets are "net importers" of product. The imports come from abroad (mostly Europe and Latin America) and from the U.S. Gulf Coast (via pipeline—mostly the Colonial line—and via tankers). The U.S.-flagged ("Jones Act") tanker fleet has been in long-term decline. Meanwhile, ever since President Ronald Reagan permitted the export of products, the Atlantic Coast and Northeast regions have had to compete with foreign markets for U.S.-produced products. Increasingly, there have been problems encountered in moving both distillate and gasoline into the Atlantic Coast market. When the pipeline is fully utilized and when imports are inadequate, there is a potential need to waive the Jones Act requirements on the U.S. product tanker fleet to enable non-U.S.-flagged vessels to carry cargoes between U.S. ports. While Jones Act waivers are available, they are rarely granted. Streamlining procedures for issuing waivers to the Jones Act would facilitate the elimination of this market anomaly and free up supply within the U.S. market during severe logistics crises.

The failure to coordinate environmental policy in a manner consistent with energy supply goals is making itself felt in the pocketbook of the American consumer. Lack of coherent policy has led to lower attention to the kinds of demand-management programs and diversification strategies that will be needed to meet the dual challenges of environmental enhancement and energy security, including fighting global warming and expanding energy demand. Continued overreliance on oil—with relative neglect of efficiency—has left the United States and other importing countries more vulnerable to disruptions in supply. With limited spare capacity, a significant accident anywhere in the world, including, for example, along Alaska's pipeline infrastructure due to an earthquake, would affect global conditions. Accidents in two or more places would be even worse. It is in this context of limited surplus capacity that concern is raised about the resources of the Middle East. Gulf crude oil comprises about 25 percent of world supply today. Many analysts project it could increase to more than 30–40 percent over the coming decade. If political factors were to block the development of new oil fields in the Middle East, the ramifications for world oil markets could be quite severe unless measures are taken immediately to diversify to other energy fuels.

International Issues
U.S. unilateral sanctions as well as multilateral sanctions against oil-producing countries have discouraged oil resource investment in a number of key oil provinces, including Iraq, Iran, and Libya. U.S. sanctions policy has constrained capacity expansion to some extent in Iran and Libya, although the unilateral aspect of the U.S. action limited its impact. In the case of Iraq, the U.N. sanctions imposed as a result of the Iraqi invasion of Kuwait have had a severe effect on potential Iraqi production.

Sanctions' role in constraining investment in several key OPEC countries has aggravated the global problem of spare production capacity, which is now less diversified among a number of large producers than was the case twenty years ago. The consequent lack of competition has contributed to high prices. Most of today's spare productive capacity is located in Saudi Arabia. And Saudi Arabia's high, and growing, level of production and the lack of significant spare unutilized capacity outside the kingdom have spotlighted that country's critical role in determining the state of current and future oil markets, in turn creating unique political pressures. Iran and Iraq accuse Saudi Arabia of seeking higher production rates to accommodate the economic interests of the

United States, Japan, and Europe at the expense of the needs of local populations, creating internal pressures in the Arabian Gulf region against a moderate price stance. Bitter perceptions in the Arab world that the United States has not been evenhanded in brokering peace negotiations between Israel and the Palestinians have exacerbated these pressures on Saudi Arabia and other Gulf Cooperation Council (GCC) countries and given political leverage to Iraq's Saddam Hussein to lobby for support among the Arab world's populations.

Several key producing countries in these important areas remain closed to investment. Encouragement of open investment policies in these countries would greatly promote renewed competition among the largest oil producers and the advancement of oil supplies in the coming years. A reopening of these areas to foreign investment could make a critical difference in providing surplus supplies to markets in the coming decade.

Removal of bureaucratic, logistical, and political obstacles to investment in Russia could also play a major role in promoting supply outside the Middle East. The deterioration of the Russian oil industry has been a prominent feature of international oil markets in recent years. While Russia has the world's eighth-largest oil reserves, the country's political and economic problems have discouraged investment by both domestic and international oil companies. As a result, oil production in Russia has fallen to about 6 million b/d in 1999, down from 12.5 million b/d in the late 1980s. Both Russia and the Caspian Basin countries show promise as key future suppliers of hydrocarbons. In fact these two regions could hold as much as 27 percent of the world's undiscovered oil resources. But, bureaucratic, logistical, and political obstacles remain a hindrance both to the timely development of currently exploitable reserves and to new discoveries.

Oil resource development in Latin America, which offers great strategic benefits to the United States, has also slowed in the past year or two as sharp declines in oil fields in Venezuela and Colombia have not been offset by new oil fields coming online. Political uncertainties in both countries are thwarting foreign investment, and state revenues are tight, discouraging spending in oil and natural gas fields by government-owned oil monopolies.

But it would be a mistake for the United States to continue to rely largely on development of key oil resources in the Middle East and Russia as the linchpin of energy policy. Instead, U.S. energy policy must also focus on reversing the decline in interest in energy efficiency and conservation at home. The experience of the 1970s has shown that energy security and energy price competition are enhanced by diversity of suppliers and of fuel choices. The economies of other countries such as Japan and Germany are better shielded from oil price changes than is the U.S. economy because of the greater emphasis on efficiency and conservation.

Unfortunately, there is no new technology available on the immediate horizon that could be commercialized for as widespread use as oil and gas in the next ten years. Promotion of renewable fuels (e.g., bio-fuels) sounds attractive and should be pursued. But even if renewable fuels use were to be doubled over the next ten years as a result of a sizable commitment to these more environmentally friendly fuels, they would still only represent a low share of both electricity and total U.S. energy use. Nuclear energy could be a clean, ample alternative for electricity but problems of waste fuels, safety, and public confidence would have to be overcome.

Similarly, industry and other groups are lobbying for the opening of the Arctic National Wildlife Refuge (ANWR) to foster energy development. This is an important issue for reasons seldom raised in current debates. Alaska oil production has entered a period of decline, which can be reversed only by opening up the ANWR. Such an opening could lead to the development of resources that could make a significant contribution to domestic supply for decades and would also bolster domestic industry and the local and national economies. While the opening of the ANWR would not in and of itself solve U.S. oil concerns, especially those related to foreign dependence, added resources would undoubtedly be significant. Yet, such a development program could take seven to ten years to implement (although industry optimists claim that an emergency effort could reduce the lag to three years) and would not free the United States from the cyclical energy supply dilemmas that keep recurring.

In sum there are no quick fix solutions to today's energy problems. Rather, a broad combination of measures is required that will stimulate investment, enhance access to new supplies of oil and gas, promote competition and eliminate political barriers to world energy markets, limit the increase in energy demand, and promote new, cleaner technologies.

Deregulation: Pluses and Minuses

Many industry representatives and specialists believe that market forces can eventually initiate many of these changes without government interference. They even argue that consumers can foster cleaner fuel preferences through the marketplace and market mechanisms. There is merit in these arguments in favor of market solutions. But energy sector deregulation and reliance on market solutions and consumer preferences can only go so far because they do not take into account critical "public goods" aspects of energy supply and environmental protection.

In the 1970s, virtually all governments in the industrial and developing worlds directly administered the prices of key energy components, both at the primary level (crude oil, natural gas) and at the consumer level (petroleum product prices, residential natural gas, and electric power). Governments were also involved in major purchase contracts for internationally traded energy commodities (oil and natural gas primarily), and often tied these contracts to other trade and national security issues (barter of oil for construction projects, soft loans, arms).

Today governments have largely retreated from the energy sector. There is a widespread global consensus that administered policies and regulations that fly in the face of market fundamentals are inefficient, impede smooth adjustment to rapidly changing times, and infuse energy issues with other political issues (in short, politicizing energy issues unnecessarily). Markets have been deregulated and liberalized; and government companies have been privatized. Wherever governments still own significant energy assets, the state-owned enterprises are generally run on com-

mercial terms. Moreover, governmental monopolies in the energy area have been broken, and national preferential considerations
have been reduced.

Generally speaking, liberalization has facilitated efficiency and
smooth allocation of resources to users who most require these
resources. But rapid deregulation of the oil, natural gas, and power
sectors has also reduced the incentives for specific businesses to
invest in large inventories or excess capacity that can help smooth
markets during times of disruption or unexpected volatility in demand
growth. Tightening environmental regulation for construction
of new energy facilities has also discouraged investment in some
locations. These changes have placed more pressure on how to achieve
the public benefits of inventory and spare production and generation capacity without discouraging investment in energy resources.
It has also changed the nature of the debate on strategic stockpiles
and government-controlled assets.

The IEA has provided an important institutional mechanism
for coordinating international preparations for such a disruption,
and its members have instituted strategic stockpiles that have, in
turn, served as a major deterrent against producer countries indi-
vidually or collectively using their "oil weapon" to pressure or
"blackmail" individual oil-importing countries. However, deregulation has brought some unintended consequences about strategic stockpiles. By and large, deregulation of energy markets has
meant that the establishment of inventories and the determina-
tion of their size have been left by governments to the market to
decide, except in the case of government-held emergency stores.
But markets do not always send fully accurate signals. That is in
part a result of lack of market transparency and the realities that
with imperfect information market participants tend to take the
short view.

More recently, the lagged interplay between supply and demand
in several energy commodities this year has caused market disruptions.
It is possible that for some of these commodities, the market
may, over time, provide its own solution, through increased refinery runs, increased gas drilling/production, and greater stimulus

for investment to increase capacity. But interventions may occur that hasten this process or ease constraints more quickly.

Inventories serve as a premier tool in preventing market failures and in managing supply dislocations. Spare petroleum or natural gas production and deliverability capacity or redundancy in power generation capacity are ultimately inventory and inventory management issues. Spare capacities reflect an inventory of available supply in case of market dislocation or unexpected disruption. Similarly, more conventional references to stores of natural gas or of petroleum products or of crude oil are also inventories. Energy markets are constantly challenged by unexpected events—from severe weather to sudden technological changes that undermine forecasts of supply and demand. Without inventory or spare capacity, such events can create extreme price volatility, sometimes for short periods of time but also sometimes for extended periods of time. Moreover, severe price volatility can become self-generating by discouraging investment by industry players who cannot properly assess future market potential.

The unanticipated consequence of deregulation, industry consolidation and restructuring, and of environmental policies on inventories is now raising new challenges for policymakers. It is also redefining the debate on the appropriate role of government intervention in energy markets. That is because of the political impact from supply shortfalls and price volatility on classes of consumers and on the general economy, when supplies are effectively auctioned to the highest bidder in times of shortage.

The Task Force's action program for implementing a coherent U.S. energy policy is framed in the context of the fundamentally changed circumstances in today's energy sector. For the two decades following the energy price spikes of the 1970s, the main opportunities and challenges for governments and consumers were based on the sometimes extraordinarily large surplus capacities that defined the energy system. These surplus capacities have now disappeared, or have been reduced to such low levels that there is only a limited cushion available to meet growth in demand or to buffer economies against disruptions. As demand moves against and away from capacity limits, the result is price volatility.

Over the past three years, the prices of most core energy sources—electricity, natural gas, and oil—have been more volatile than at any time in recent history. At a global level, crude oil prices hit their highest and lowest levels since the price collapse of the mid-1980s between 1998 and 2000, with the exception of a brief price spike after Iraq invaded Kuwait in 1990. In North America, natural gas prices this winter set all-time record highs, and may well do so again a year from now, while electricity prices have reached unprecedented peaks in California and other pockets of the United States. Other regions of the country are likely to suffer the same fate this summer.

Under these circumstances, history demonstrates that the main tasks of energy policy are the following:

- to assure that markets operate efficiently so as to develop the infrastructure necessary to meet growing requirements of demand;
- to facilitate orderly growth in demand;
- to ensure the well-being of the human habitat and ecosystem; and
- to guarantee that mechanisms are in place for warding off and, if necessary, for managing disruptions to energy supply.

FINDINGS

This report is motivated by the belief—shared by many energy specialists—that pervasive shortages in the energy sector will not go away of their own accord, other than through a sharp economic downturn. Market solutions are fundamental to providing the kind of stable and predictable energy prices that are needed to sustain the economy and safeguard security over the long term, and they should be embraced. But market solutions go only so far, especially at a time when inventories of all sorts are so low as to result in price surges that harm consumers and cause political backlash. A more comprehensive strategic approach is needed.

Implementing this reinvigorated energy policy will take time. Quick fixes can alleviate supply bottlenecks or conserve energy use, but the energy sector is capital intensive and, with few noteworthy exceptions, involves projects that can unfold only within a three- to five-year horizon, or even one that is even longer.

Energy issues need to be brought before the public to counter some widespread misconceptions. There are no easy, overnight, and politically attractive solutions to the country's or the world's infrastructure and supply problems. There is no existing technology that can quickly replace oil in the crucial transportation sector. There is no place at home or abroad where enough oil or gas can be developed fast enough to moderate prices in the next six to twelve months. There is no cost-free way to allow unrestricted energy use and simultaneously safeguard the environment. But neither is the world running out of energy resources.

The Task Force acknowledges that energy policy starts at home. But any attempt to reframe U.S. energy policy must take into account the fact that the energy sector has become extremely interdependent internationally. The United States cannot achieve energy independence without the emergence of new technologies that are not yet on the horizon. Increasing domestic supplies will therefore not necessarily reduce U.S. vulnerability to disruptions to any substantial extent, and artificial ceilings or targets for imports will contribute little to security and could create unwanted distortions. An oil shortfall anywhere in the world will produce an equal price rise in every country, irrespective of the level of national import dependence, as long as markets are allowed to clear without government interference.

The United States must face up to this energy interdependence squarely and pursue new paths to assure that neither its economy nor policies are excessively vulnerable to foreign influence. For the foreseeable future, the Gulf will remain the world's base-load supplier and least expensive source of oil to meet growing demand. The global nature of oil trade and pricing means that it matters little if Gulf oil flows to Asia or to the United States. Middle East Gulf pricing and supply trends will affect energy costs around the globe regardless. If the United States wishes to change this reality, it must start now to deploy new energy technologies that will lessen this dependence in the long run.

The Task Force determined ten broad findings:

1. *The U.S. government has not for a long time adequately integrated the security, energy, technological, financial, and environmental policies that make up a comprehensive energy policy.* It has relied on overlapping commercial and political interests with key oil-producing countries to meet the needs of its own economy and those of the international economy. A surplus in energy supplies during the past two decades convinced policymakers that other objectives could take precedence over energy security and that the costs of neglect would remain low. That period has ended. In today's tighter energy markets, the costs of leaving energy security unattended could become extremely high. These costs, and the means of reducing them, need to be evaluated in a more purposeful, strategic fashion.

2. *There are no overnight solutions to the energy supply and infrastructure bottlenecks facing the nation and the world.* Success will require long-term investments. It will also require the revocation of failed, outmoded, or simply less impor-

tant policies, which interfere with the pursuit of energy security. Economic sanctions that limit energy investment and environmental policies that increase the costs or availability of energy sources require a fair-minded review. A few concrete short-term actions are available, but many of these clash with other policy objectives, which may need to be compromised or even scrapped.

3. *Continuous governmental review of the trade-offs between energy security and other national goals is needed.* The articulation of a coherent energy policy requires the integration of foreign, national security, and trade policy with numerous domestic environmental, tax, and investment programs. Energy policy should play a significant role in diplomatic discourse, especially where bilateral relations with major powers are concerned. (See Appendix B.)

4. *Environmental issues affecting energy policy require new approaches at home and abroad.* The American public cares as much as the citizens of other countries about such issues as greenhouse gases and other atmospheric emissions, underground leakage of noxious substances, and other environmental dangers. Sensible energy policy must take this into account. But it is important that the public understand that enhanced environmental standards come at a price to the availability and cost of fuels. It is equally important that the public understand the environmental and public-health consequences of unfettered energy consumption. The government should take a leadership role in fostering such understanding. Also, better coordination of fuels standards is needed, both inside the United States and with U.S. trading partners.

5. *Energy infrastructure can be rebuilt and expanded rapidly only if the government actively facilitates private-sector decision-making and investment.* The government should pave the way by removing unnecessary jurisdictional and other obstacles to construction and enlargement of pipelines, power plants, the electricity grid, and other infrastructure. It also needs to weigh the desirability of incentives to accel-

erate the development of spare infrastructure and the accumulation of inventory to alleviate supply disruptions.

6. *U.S. energy independence is not attainable. Policy must therefore focus on increasing the number of energy suppliers, the
   kinds of energy consumed, and the efficiency with which energy is used.* The effort should include renewable and nonconventional forms of energy, as well as conventional fuels,
   while recognizing that even a doubling of renewable fuel supplies by 2020 could result in renewables having a lower
   share of the market than today. Oil supply-side policy
   should take into account the danger of relying on Middle
   East producers for all of the world's spare capacity without
   also bolstering strategic stockpiles and reviewing rules for
   their use.

7. *Persistently tight crude oil markets highlight the concentration of resources in the Middle East Gulf region and the
   vulnerability of the global economy to domestic conditions
   in the key producer countries.* The Gulf nations have one
   major asset—their oil and gas reserves. They, like Russia,
   Mexico, Indonesia, Nigeria, Venezuela, and some other oil-
   producing nations, depend heavily on hydrocarbons to
   support their citizens. If the current regimes in the Gulf cannot deliver a better standard of living for rapidly increasing
   populations, social upheaval could result, and anti-Western
   elements could gain power. Similar concerns exist with
   respect to some other oil-producing countries outside the Gulf.

8. *Energy policy has underplayed energy efficiency and demand-
   management measures for two decades.* It is clear that vigorous demand management could significantly lower the volume
   of energy required for economic growth. Demand curbs could
   apply to residential, commercial, and industrial uses, but they
   are likely to bring the greatest and fastest benefits in the core
   transportation sector.

9. *The instruments available to deal with energy-supply disruptions are increasingly inadequate to the tasks they need
   to manage.* To date, the keystone to managing emergency
   supply disruptions has been the Strategic Petroleum Reserve.

The International Energy Agency and its policies, including building of strategic reserves of crude oil and petroleum products and mechanisms to share available supplies in times of disruption, play an important role, as well. But this program addresses yesterday's needs. IEA members' oil consumption has stagnated, while demand has grown rapidly outside, causing the agency to lose the critical mass necessary for managing a future shortfall. The size and effectiveness of the ninety-day cushion mandated by the IEA also needs to be reexamined, as does management of the SPR, particularly by bringing in modern financial tools to help build the reserve with minimal impact on government budgets. Finally, what constitutes an energy supply shortfall needs to be redefined in light of changes in the structure of the global oil market.

10. *The United States needs to articulate a new vision of how best to manage international energy interdependence, one that promotes market transparency and fair distribution of gains from increased trade and investment.* Fundamental information about market trends is often unavailable. Energy producers and consumers need to find ways to build common institutions. Unless the U.S. government provides leadership in modernizing market and investment structures, there is a clear danger that others will take the reins and develop institutions that run counter to U.S. interests.

STRATEGIC POLICY CHOICES

For two decades, the United States has gone without a serious energy policy. In the past, such complacency about energy could be justified because world supplies appeared to be indefinitely ample.
The myth of plenty was reinforced by the enormous gains that were
made as market forces were allowed to work, as regulations and
controls were eliminated, and as energy prices fell in real terms across
the world. These gains, in turn, allowed U.S. leaders—both
Republican and Democratic—to take a minimalist approach sup-
ported by the comfort of consensus politics that reflected an
avoidance of strategic choices. From the perspective of this Task
Force, there is no escaping the fact that we are reaching the
beginning of an extensive period of sporadic supply shortages and
periodic price hikes in the United States and in other parts of the
world. This new situation requires a reevaluation of U.S. policy
approaches. The United States faces three policy paths: first, continue the easy approach of "muddling through" with marginal Strategic Petroleum Reserve management and complete free market
solutions; second, take a near-term, narrow approach by expanding supply to ensure cheap energy while enduring conflict with interest groups; or third, develop a comprehensive and balanced energy
security policy with near-term actions and long-term initiatives
addressing supply-side and demand-side policy instruments and
diversification of energy supply resources that enables the United States to escape from a pattern of recurring energy crises.

TAKING THE EASY APPROACH

Clearly the path of maintaining the status quo of no energy policy is by far the easiest short-term option. This is obviously the
path of least resistance. Under such an approach, very little initiative would be needed and could be limited to a very circumspect

focus: reviewing the size and mechanisms associated with the SPR and its coordinated use with other countries in the International Energy Agency. This limited policy would dictate that the United States simply muddle through any portending crisis that might occur by reducing the pain of such an actual event through the use of emergency measures at the time of the event.

It is a path that could readily be chosen for two reasons. First, there is the ever-present hope that the market, left to its own devices, will eventually correct itself and overcome current supply problems. Secondly, history seems to justify this approach. Major oil disruptions with serious consequences seem to occur only every decade or so, it can be argued, seemingly limiting the costs of doing nothing. Electric power shortages will eventually get sorted out, and in any case states rather than the federal government bear the brunt of citizens' claims. This approach obviates the need to tackle the difficult political issues that would have to be resolved to forge an energy policy consensus in Congress. No comprehensive policy means Congress does not have to make the compromises required to enact the legislation to backstop a more effective, comprehensive approach.

One clear benefit of this approach is that the short-term costs to the consumer would be limited and that no hard sacrifices would have to be made. The costs to U.S. taxpayers seem minimal and indirect and in any event they can be postponed. Consumers have the prospect of the market assisting them yet again in achieving low energy costs. Some of the real costs, such as the high-cost U.S. military presence in the Middle East, are already accepted and forgotten by the public.

But the problem is that there is overwhelming evidence that there will be no "free lunch" for taxpayers. A disruption might well occur at a time when the mechanisms for dealing with it have become outmoded, too narrowly confined to too narrow a segment of the world community to make a difference. And meanwhile, the market volatility of the past few years may be a precursor of much worse to come—a roller coaster of prices confusing the investment climate and impeding the marshaling of capital required to overcome supply obstacles whose emergence triggered the new critical state to begin with.

Under this scenario, the United States remains a prisoner of its energy dilemma, suffering on a recurring basis from the negative consequences of sporadic energy shortages. These consequences can include recession, social dislocation of the poorest Americans, and at the extremes, a need for military intervention. Moreover, this approach leaves festering the conflict between rising energy demand and its potentially devastating impact on the global environment.

TAKING A SUPPLY-SIDE APPROACH

Another easy-to-digest approach would be one that focuses predominantly on supply-side solutions. A supply-side perspective is attractive because it offers some eventual reprieve from the negative impacts of energy shortages but with little or no direct cost or sacrifice to the average American. A supply-side approach would aim to increase the amount of land available in the United States and around the world for resource exploration and exploitation and offer whatever tax or other incentives would be needed to stimulate greater investment in energy assets. The Task Force agrees that the supply side is an essential focal point of any workable policy solution. Indeed, the Task Force recommendations incorporate a number of supply-side options, including both conventional and nonconventional fuels. But the Task Force does not endorse an exclusively supply-side approach for a number of reasons.

To begin, the costs of this policy are that it almost certainly will bring its designers into conflict with public interest groups, especially those that support environmental protection and land management. This will create an atmosphere where the American people might feel forced to make a difficult choice between a cleaner environment or ample energy supplies. Partisan politicians are already driving this perception by comments in the media or through partisan bills in Congress. But no such choice might be required over the long term if a more integrative, comprehensive approach were to be chosen. Environmental protection and energy policy do not have to be decoupled, but they can be integrally linked through smart policy choices.

Another problem with a supply-side approach is that it creates the impression that cheap energy is an inalienable right and is available in the very near term. This creates an incentive to greater consumption that is not likely to be sustainable and will eventually net us back to shortages and price volatility once again.

TAKING A COMPREHENSIVE APPROACH TO ENERGY SECURITY

Thus, it is the view of this Task Force that only by forging a comprehensive energy policy can the United States escape from a pattern of recurring energy crises. It is a tenet of the Task Force that a workable and comprehensive energy policy requires a balance of supply-side and demand-side policy instruments if it is to attract a practicable operating congressional majority in the United States. Such a policy would favor diversification of energy supply by fuel and by source.

The recommendations of this Task Force represent its best attempts to outline a more coherent and comprehensive outlook for a long-term policy initiative that also takes into account immediate steps. Thus, the recommendations contained in this report are intended to be considered as a whole. Outlined supply-side options require simultaneous pursuit of the demand-management instruments enumerated by the Task Force. Combining them provides a powerful mechanism for enhancing the energy security of American citizens.

By way of one simple example, it might well be the case that enhancing exploration and exploitation of hydrocarbon resources of the North Slope of Alaska might well uncover new resources that could substantially reduce U.S. dependence on imports. But the Arctic National Wildlife Reserve is unlikely to achieve needed support for permitting the access of companies to its exploitation in the absence of strong demand-side measures. As the report indicates, demand-side measures could, alone, have even greater and less costly an impact on America's medium-term balance of fundamentals than a supply-side only policy. And a combination of the two, of new supplies and of lower demand, in all likelihood provides a more durable solution.

A truly comprehensive policy may well provide the kinds of balance and compromise that are consistent with much of America's political history. However, any comprehensive plan is likely to require confrontation with other policy objectives that have deep constituencies. In some measure, concessions will have to be made that will impinge on certain local environment goals, states rights, Middle East policy, economic sanctions policy, Russia policy, and hemispheric and international trade policy. Making compromises could be politically painful and will require sustained leadership from the highest levels of government.

But the benefits will be quite real. The comprehensive approach could minimize the negative consequences of a disruption in any particular fuel and help shield the American consumer from the painful effects of the cyclical nature of the energy business. It might allow us to reduce military spending down the road and to create export opportunities for American firms through the development of clean energy technologies. It might also allow us to experience sustained economic growth but without perilous environmental consequences.

The Task Force offers a detailed discussion of the components of a comprehensive approach with elaboration about the policy trade-offs required for such an initiative.

STRATEGY

To ensure America's well-being and economic prosperity in this new era of energy constraints, the United States must have a strategic energy policy predicated on a clear vision of the requirements of energy security. This vision must reflect domestic economic and environmental considerations, as well as geopolitical trends and security imperatives. It is vital for the United States to assure stable and transparent international energy markets that provide prices which foster economic growth. It is also in the strategic interest of the United States to assure that appropriate national and international mechanisms are in place to prevent disruptions in energy supplies where possible, and to manage efficiently and equitably any disruption that might occur. To this end, the United States should promote a global network of arrangements that protects against disruption, while securing equitable mechanisms for burden-sharing if required.

Given the magnitude of the potential threat represented by global climate change, it is equally in the strategic interest of the United States to identify and implement cost-effective measures at home and abroad to stabilize the atmospheric concentration of greenhouse gases at levels that will not lead to catastrophic climatic change.

Many different constituencies within the U.S. government will need to work together to develop a unified and integrated energy policy framework with well-defined and orchestrated goals—a policy that will address not only today's energy bottlenecks, but also will seek to provide affordable, clean, and reliable energy supplies five to fifteen years into the future, in order to underpin long-term economic growth in an environmentally acceptable

[39]

manner and to promote the security of the United States and its allies.

Strategy is about making choices among competing goals. In reaching the appropriate balance, U.S. energy policy must take into account the fact that the vigor with which environmental goals are pursued will affect the costs of energy supplies. Equally, the policy needs to consider that the vigorous pursuit of market-oriented solutions can diminish the level of consumer and general economic protection from the negative effects of price volatility. Finally, the goal of affordable, clean, and reliable energy supply places some constraints on and is influenced by U.S. diplomacy and strategic policy.

The Task Force developed a broad consensus on the following strategic goals for the nation's energy policy:

1. Protecting and promoting long-term diversity of affordable energy supply for sustained global economic growth. Diversity refers both to the mix of energy sources and the geographic origin of that energy. The priorities established among fuels should take into account environmental objectives, fuel efficiency, and national security considerations.

2. Promoting energy end-use efficiency as a near-term approach to meeting economic, security, and environmental goals.

3. Providing adequate safeguards, both at home and abroad, against energy supply disruptions and against manipulation of markets by any party, state or private.

4. Promoting market forces wherever and whenever possible, while acting to ensure order in case of market failures or severe shortfalls or accidents. Market failures can involve interference in trade flows by private or state-owned entities and actions by adversaries. They can also involve flaws in regulatory structures, including environmental regulations.

5. Creating a stable, competitive, and predictable investment climate to ensure that energy resources and infrastructure expand to meet the growing needs of the world's population in a manner that safeguards the environment, pro-

motes consumer needs, and enables U.S. companies to operate on an even playing field.

6. Encouraging competition in the United States and abroad, to the benefit of both U.S. consumers and companies.

7. Ensuring that all citizens, and particularly less affluent Americans, have access to reliable and affordable basic heating fuels and electricity when markets fail to serve this critical function.

RECOMMENDATIONS

The recommendations of the Task Force are divided into two sections. The first comprises actions to be considered in the very short term to assure that appropriate mechanisms are in place to deal with potential supply disruptions and to buffer the economy from adverse impacts of price volatility. The second set of recommendations is longer term in nature. The first set of recommendations concerns action items designed to provide the government with "breathing space" in case of shortfalls or emergencies. The second set concerns a framework for dealing with the challenges of creating new supplies and ample capacities along various linked global energy supply chains, while also preserving and enhancing the human habitat.

IMMEDIATE STEPS

1. **Deter and Manage International Supply Shortfalls**
   Recent oil market-price volatility has been driven by a number of complex factors. However, three key drivers continue to fuel upward pressure on prices: OPEC policy and the organization's lack of spare productive capacity; the policies of Iraq and concerns about the reliability of its U.N.-monitored oil exports; and fears of a possible flare-up in the Arab-Israeli conflict. These factors have created uncertainty in markets that has at various times outweighed considerations of immediate market supply availability, fueling speculation and pushing prices above $30–$35 a barrel at various times in recent months. Although these situations cannot be solved overnight, certain steps could be considered to ameliorate their negative impact on oil market stability.
   a. *Develop a diplomatic program ensuring GCC allies remain prepared and willing to maintain stable prices to promote global economic growth and also to fill any unexpected*

supply shortfalls in times of turmoil in the oil markets, whether created by accident or by the adverse political actions by any producing nation. The vast majority of all unused, spare oil productive capacity is located in Saudi Arabia and the United Arab Emirates. It appears that Kuwait might soon be added to that list. Saudi Arabia has over 1 million b/d of spare sustainable capacity and considerably more surge capacity that could be brought online for several weeks in a crisis. The UAE has some limited spare capacity of several hundred thousand barrels a day. Kuwait might soon have a similar amount. These are all very important countries for the United States, with a fundamentally positive attitude toward cooperation and support, and with the only meaningful spare production capacity in the world. They all deserve being cultivated as special priorities of U.S. policy.

Over the past year, Iraq has effectively become a swing producer, turning its taps on and off when it has felt such action was in its strategic interest to do so. Saudi Arabia has proven willing to provide replacement supplies to the market when Iraqi exports have been reduced. This role has been extremely important in avoiding greater market volatility and in countering Iraq's efforts to take advantage of the oil market's structure. Saudi Arabia's role in this needs to be preserved, and should not be taken for granted. There is domestic pressure on the GCC leaders to reject cooperation to cool oil markets during times of a shortfall in Iraqi oil production. These populations are dissatisfied with the "no-fly zone" bombing and the sanctions regime against Iraq, perceived U.S. bias in the Arab-Israeli peace process, and lack of domestic economic pressures. A diplomatic dialogue that emphasizes common U.S.-GCC goals and programs should be pursued at the highest levels to minimize the potential for tension over these other issues. Goodwill efforts such as a U.S. offer to buy oil from spare capacity for the Strategic Petroleum Reserve when market circumstances warrant and a willingness to discuss coordinated response to supply emergencies can be used to offset anti-American sentiment among elite groups in these countries.

There are, however, some trade-off issues. Working together with the GCC could restrict some of the United States's freedom of movement on security and foreign policy actions that might be desirable with regard to Iraq or the Arab-Israeli conflict from a U.S. point of view.

b. *Prepare for contingencies and gain agreement on coordination in the IEA in efforts to deal with any attempts by adversaries to remove oil from international markets.* Some European country positions on economic sanctions against Iraq differ from the U.S. position, most notably France but also some other IEA countries including Japan. Still, the IEA must be assured of efficient joint decision-making in the event of a supply disruption under tight market conditions. This includes any possibility that Saddam Hussein may remove Iraqi oil from the market for an extended period of time and that Saudi Arabia will not or cannot replace all of the barrels. (This is a contingency that hangs over the market given the ability of Baghdad to continue to earn revenues through smuggling and other uncontrolled oil exports, even if it officially cuts off exports that are permitted through U.N. procedures.) IEA member countries should be in agreement in advance of such an event on what joint actions it will take. The IEA has been very successful in recent years in providing definitive and forceful statements of its intentions, and these statements have improved the maintenance of orderly markets. The administration needs to ensure that recent events do not derail this past success.

c. *Minimize public conflicts with OPEC and other independent oil-exporting countries but emphasize importance of market factors in setting prices.* The previous administration engaged in public exchanges with OPEC over the producer organization's decisions to push oil prices higher. This fueled anti-American sentiment among certain sectors of the population in the Middle East, lent support to the claims of Saddam Hussein, and brought pressures on some U.S.-friendly regimes in the region. The United States needs to prevent aggravation of this situation by avoiding public discussion of the targeting of particular price goals and emphasizing common interests of promoting and protecting growth in the global economy. Such growth maintains demand for OPEC's oil. Rather than specify a price level that is "good for the United States"—which creates an "us-against-you" mindset on oil-pricing policy—the United States should emphasize as a first line of policy its position that market forces should be left to set the price of oil. Specific discussion of price should be kept to private diplomatic discussion whenever possible. Although short-term political gains can be garnered at home in the United States for jawboning OPEC, longer term this activity is likely to stimulate more entrenched positions within that organization, leading to higher oil prices and eventually wearing down any short-term public relations benefit inside the United States.

d. *While moving to defuse tensions in the Arab-Israeli conflict through conflict resolution and negotiations, maintain energy and political issues in U.S.–Middle East relations on separate tracks.* The timing might not be appropriate for a major initiative to solve the Arab-Israeli conflict in a comprehensive manner, but it is important to reduce immediate tensions and violence in that conflict. While this is a tenet of U.S. foreign policy for other reasons, it can also be helpful to the oil situation in ensuring that the two issues do not become linked and are kept on separate tracks. Iraq has been engaged in a clever public relations campaign to intersect these two issues and stir up anti-American sentiment inside and outside the Middle East. The bombing of Iraq by the U.S.-led coalition in February 2001 spurred anti-U.S. demonstrations in support of Iraq in traditional U.S. allies such as Egypt. Moreover, Saddam Hussein is trying to recast himself as the champion of the Palestinian cause to some success among young Palestinians. Any severe violence in the West Bank, Gaza, or southern Lebanon will give Iraq more leverage in its efforts to discredit the United States and U.S. intentions. A focus on the anti-Israeli sympathies of some Arab oil-producing countries diverts attention from the repressive nature of the Iraqi regime. Instead it rewards Iraq in its claim to Arab leadership for "standing up to the United States for ten years." Israel will assert its right to defend itself from terrorist or other attacks, so it is important that both sides of the Arab-Israeli conflict are given a stake in avoiding conflict and violence. Creating an atmosphere where both sides are willing to show restraint can be an important goal for U.S. diplomacy on this issue.

e. *Review policies toward Iraq with the aim to lowering anti-Americanism in the Middle East and elsewhere, and set the groundwork to eventually ease Iraqi oil-field investment restrictions.* Iraq remains a destabilizing influence to U.S. allies in the Middle East, as well as to regional and global order, and to the flow of oil to international markets from the Middle East. Saddam Hussein has also demonstrated a willingness to threaten to use the oil weapon and to use his own export program to manipulate oil markets. This would display his personal power, enhance his image as a "Pan-Arab" leader supporting the Palestinians against Israel, and pressure others for a lifting of economic sanctions against his regime.

The United States should conduct an immediate policy review toward Iraq, including military, energy, economic, and political/diplomatic assessments. The United States should then develop an integrated strategy with key allies in Europe and Asia and with key countries in the Middle East to restate the goals with respect to Iraqi policy and to restore a cohesive coalition of key allies. Goals should be designed in a realistic fashion, and they should be clearly and consistently stated and defended to revive U.S. credibility on this issue. Actions and policies to promote these goals should endeavor to enhance the well-being of the Iraqi people. Sanctions that are not effective should be phased out and replaced with highly focused and enforced sanctions that target the regime's ability to maintain and acquire weapons of mass destruction. A new plan of action should be developed to use diplomatic and other means to support U.N. Security Council efforts to build a strong arms-control regime to stem the flow of arms and controlled substances into Iraq. Policy should rebuild coalition cooperation on this issue, while emphasizing the common interest in security. This issue of arms sales to Iraq should be brought near the top of the agenda for dialogue with China and Russia.

Once an arms-control program is in place, the United States could consider reducing restrictions on oil investments inside Iraq. Like it or not, Iraqi reserves represent a major asset that can quickly add capacity to world oil markets and inject a more competitive tenor to oil trade. However, such a policy will be quite costly as this trade-off will encourage Saddam Hussein to boast of his "victory" against the United States, fuel his ambitions, and potentially strengthen his regime. Once so encouraged and if his access to oil revenues were to be increased by adjustments in oil sanctions, Saddam Hussein could be a greater security threat to U.S. allies in the region if weapons of mass destruction (WMD) sanctions, weapons regimes, and the coalition against him are not strengthened. Still, the maintenance of continued oil sanctions is becoming increasingly difficult to implement. Moreover, Saddam Hussein has many means of gaining revenues, and the sanctions regime helps perpetuate his lock on the country's economy.

Another problem with easing restrictions on the Iraqi oil industry to allow greater investment is that GCC allies of the United States will not like to see Iraq gain larger market share in international oil markets. In fact, even Russia could lose from having sanctions eased on Iraq, because Russian companies now benefit from exclusive contracts and Iraqi export capacity is restrained, supporting the price of oil and raising the value of Russian oil exports. If sanctions covering Iraq's oil sector were eased and Iraq benefited from infrastructure improvements, Russia might lose its competitive position inside Iraq, and also oil prices might fall over time, hurting the Russian economy. These issues will have to be discussed in bilateral exchanges.

2. Remove Bottlenecks and Other Obstacles to Energy Supply, Both Domestically and Internationally

There are few options available to the United States to expand supply in the short run whether or not there are energy supply shortfalls. There are even fewer options available to reduce short-term demand. Fortunately, in the area of petroleum, the government has a fairly robust strategic reserve. But beyond petroleum, the options are severely limited. It is in this context that the Task Force recommends that the government consider all possible means of de-bottlenecking supplies and removing obstacles to delivery of supplies, both domestically and internationally. Options need to be considered that are unilateral as well as those that are bilateral, regional, and international or multinational by nature. In addition, the government needs to establish permanent machinery for integrating energy policy with economic, environmental, and foreign policy on a sustained basis.

Virtually all domestically available raw-material energy resources are being produced that can be. In fact, there are virtually no actions that can be taken in the short term to increase these home-grown supplies. However, there are significant obstacles to the production and distribution of certain petroleum products, gasoline in particular and distillates to a lesser extent, that have come about due to localized differences in regulations concerning petroleum product-quality specifications. These differences are related in some cases to the implementation of the Clean Air Act in areas with particularly troublesome pollution levels or because of regional preferences as discussed in the introduction to this report. These boutique fuels and the "Balkanization" that they create in the market hinder efficiency and promote shortfalls in local markets even when surplus products of other specifications might be available nearby.

What can be done to deal with market Balkanization? In general, the federal government should attempt to find ways to increase its flexibility in dealing with market anomalies that stem from product specifications and to increase product standardization so as to reduce the pernicious impacts of lack of standardization.

Such actions involve steps to be taken both at home and abroad (see below).

   a. *Streamline procedures for waiving product specifications.* A permanent interagency task force needs to be created involving, at a minimum, officials from the Department of Energy and the Environmental Protection Agency (EPA) to review the impact of boutique product specifications on regional markets within the country. It should be empowered to take action expeditiously to waive or ease mandated specifications for limited periods of time so that market dislocations can be managed.

   There are a number of tradeoffs that need to be considered. Clearly, the suspension of mandated standards could set back the achievement of national, regional, or state environmental goals. Waivers of product standards that are issued in order to enhance supply should explicitly address the continued commitment to the environmental objectives in the original regulations as well as the temporary nature of the waiver. In addition, there are potential inequities to industry: waiving certain standards could "punish" companies that had invested in new equipment and technology to meet product specification requirements and that stand to benefit from any increase in prices for their rare product. Such inequities could be remedied in the longer term through tax policy favoring those who complete costly investments.

   b. *Establish procedures to grant Jones Act waivers without adversely affecting U.S. ship owners or U.S. labor.* As discussed in the introduction to this report, U.S.-manufactured petroleum products are transported mainly by domestic pipeline or by ship but under federal mandate only U.S.-flagged ships can be used for these deliveries. For a long time the Jones Act tanker fleet was in long-term decline, but U.S. flag owners and operators have invested significant amounts of money to build vessels in the United States to comply with the Jones Act. When the pipeline is fully utilized and when imports are inadequate as was experienced last winter in New England, there is a potential need to waive the Jones

Act requirements on the U.S. product tanker fleet to enable non-U.S.-flagged vessels to carry cargoes between U.S. ports. As long as the current law exists, the government needs to send a strong signal that under no circumstances will it provide a Jones Act waiver on purely economic grounds. This is needed to give U.S. tanker owners the ability to recover costs associated with U.S.-built tankers and remove any investment uncertainty. But when the U.S. government is concerned with logistics issues, officials could signal that waivers would be granted for foreign-flagged vessels to enter the trade on an emergency, case-by-case basis when no vessels could be made available on the spot market by U.S. owners. Similar issues concern labor, which has an interest in both the manufacture and manning of the Jones Act fleet. While Jones Act waivers are available, the procedures to accomplish this are cumbersome and the waivers are rarely granted. Streamlining procedures for issuing waivers to the Jones Act would facilitate the elimination of this market anomaly and free up supply within the U.S. market during severe logistics crises.

c. *Enact legislation for federal primacy over state regulations, especially with respect to product specifications and pipeline right of way.* Ways need to be created to simplify the nation's total petroleum product slate in order to reduce market Balkanization and therefore ease localized product-supply shortages and related price volatility.

There is little doubt that establishing the primacy of federal regulations would remove a significant bottleneck to future regional supply glitches in this as in other areas. For example, it would enable the federal government to override the objections of individual states to exploration and development in offshore acreage. It could also expedite procedures involved in the siting of new or expanded energy infrastructure, including new pipelines, refineries, or power plants.

If the federal government wants to make a serious effort to foster market transparency, facilitate the development of new supplies, and expedite permitting for new energy infrastructure, legislation mandating federal primacy over state legislation and regulations in specific areas should be a very high priority. However, there are major obstacles to enacting this legislation.

- Federal legislation would almost certainly be opposed by many states, whose legislatures and elected governors have enacted product specifications that are different from and at times more stringent than federally mandated specifications.
- Federal legislation could be challenged as unconstitutional.
- In the case of some boutique fuels, local authorities have mandated them in order to help their urban areas meet national Clean Air Act targets or targets of their own that are even more stringent. Such conflicts would have to be managed by structured cooperation among the EPA, federal agencies responsible for product standards, and local officials.
- In efforts to mandate federal primacy, the administration might well feel compelled to find a middle ground for quality specifications that are significantly less stringent than what many state governments would find acceptable. Conversely, if the federal standards were to be strict enough to assist the most polluted urban areas, product quality standards and compliance costs would be unsuitably high and unnecessarily costly for regions with less severe air quality problems.

d. *Enact legislation to facilitate regional solutions to a variety of energy challenges.* Mechanisms that would be far less intrusive of the authority of state governments and regulatory bodies could be created via regional approaches. Unlike legislation mandating the primacy of federal regulations, the federal government could urge and facilitate collaborative approaches that would provide federal incentives for states that decide to work together on regional solutions. Regional approaches would be far preferable to state-only approaches in a variety of areas, including larger regional frameworks for mandating fuel specifications, emissions limits, and for establishing siting requirements for new energy infrastructure. Regional councils should be established and mandated to work in a streamlined manner with federal agencies including the EPA, the Federal Energy Regulatory Commission, and the Departments of Energy and Commerce on a variety of permitting issues.

While regional solutions would be less efficient than national solutions in eliminating bottlenecks to supply, they may in the end be more readily acceptable, since they would lend the appearance of greater local control.

e. *Investigate whether any changes to U.S. policy would quickly facilitate higher exports of oil from the Caspian Basin region.* Generally speaking, all oil-producing countries outside of OPEC are producing at maximum rates. There are a few exceptions where political problems block immediate shipments, such as pipeline problems in Colombia, where guerrilla warfare against the government extends to attacks on oil installations. Also included in this category are labor unrest and investment disputes that slow the progress of developing and producing oil in Nigeria—or Norway, for that matter. The U.S. government should assist with resolution of these problems, but a quick resolution is unlikely.

However, the exports from some oil discoveries in the Caspian Basin could be hastened if a secure, economical export route could be identified swiftly. It is unclear how much oil could be thereby released: estimates range from a relatively insignificant 10,000 b/d to well over 100,000 b/d. To this end, the administration should review policies toward this region. The option exists to downplay diplomatic activities that dictate certain geopolitical goals for specific transportation routes for Caspian oil in favor of immediate commercial solutions that may be sought by individual oil companies for short-term exports of "early" oil, including exports through Iran. These geopolitical goals can later be articulated for longer-term pipeline routing questions into the next decade.

The administration, of course, needs to take into account the tradeoffs of this policy shift. Some European companies might choose to send more oil via Iran. U.S. companies may seek case-by-case waivers to send oil through Iran that would otherwise not be produced, thus effectively forcing the United States to consider signaling a change in its policy toward Iran. In any event, the United States might find other reasons to improve relations with Iran. For example, Iran could serve as a regional counterweight to Iraq. A shift in pipeline strategy to favor commerciality might also encourage some regional Caspian players to seek a closer relationship with Russia in order to facilitate the movement of oil through Russian routes. Russia may interpret this policy as one showing weakness of resolve and a green light to press Georgia and other neighboring states to compromise their sovereignty in favor of Moscow's interests. Still, it remains unclear whether these potentially adverse developments might occur regardless of U.S. policy toward pipeline routes. In general, for strategic reasons related to U.S.-Russian relations, the United States might want to move the Caspian region into a zone of cooperation with Russia, instead of a zone of competition or confrontation. (It might seek this, for example, in order to jointly counter the rise of radical, Islamic militant elements in the region.) This arena of discussion could thus start with energy issues and later move on to other issues. Finally, U.S. insistence on the longer and costly Baku-Ceyhan pipeline route could jeopardize a more comprehensive approach toward the export of the Caspian Basin's resources and would put at risk a more commercial approach.

3. Take a Fresh Approach to Building and Maintaining National Strategic and Commercial Crude Oil and Petroleum Product Inventories

There is no doubt that the most important mechanisms for dealing with supply shortfalls are inventories of crude oil and petroleum product held both by the government and by commercial enterprises. Inventories, especially strategic stores, provide the nation's first line of defense against a supply shortfall and therefore warrant immediate attention. Nor is there any doubt that the level of crude oil and seasonal product inventories has become a significant domestic political issue. For example, there was a strikingly widespread consensus nationwide when the Northeast Heating Oil Reserve was created last year, although there were questions raised about whether this should be managed by government or by industry (with the latter through tax incentives). With respect to inventories, the Task Force has a series of recommendations.

   a. *Review the size and financing of the Strategic Petroleum Reserve.* The SPR represents the best means of replacing lost barrels of crude oil. Its ideal size relative to the size of imports has not been officially reviewed in two decades. Meanwhile, the SPR has declined both as a share of imports and in absolute size since the mid-1990s. At its peak, the SPR covered more than eighty days of imports; today it covers under fifty days. The administration should, as a high priority, review what the ideal size of the reserve should be, given the fundamental changes in the nature of disruptions that the country confronts. The review should take place both as a national, stand-alone issue and in conjunction with an international review. (See the section on longer-term issues, below.) For example, the administration may choose to make its decision about the ideal size of the SPR in consultation not only with other IEA members, but also in consultation with key OPEC producer countries. The administration should also review how it should finance reserve additions. Ideally this might be accomplished through direct budgetary allocations. At a minimum the government should aim to fill all of the nearly 700 million barrels of capacity it currently has available.

   It should be recognized that one problem with trying to refill the reserve at this time when markets are strong is that any purchases made by the U.S. government (or other consuming countries) would add to the current tight supply of international oil markets. Also, critics of the reserve may argue

that it hasn't been necessary to tap a full draw-down sir.
its creation, arguing against the need for a full ninety-da,
supply. Thus, other, more creative measures might be advised
for filling the reserve during times of temporary market weakness. One option would be to make such purchases through
a bilateral arrangement with a key oil supplier of the United States, again at a time when markets soften. The purchases
could be designed to help an oil-producing ally maintain oil
sales during a time of market weakness. Another would entail
buying oil that an OPEC country might otherwise have held
back from the market as part of its market-maintenance, pro-
duction-quota agreement. Such arrangements would have
the benefit of demonstrating U.S. support for positive con-
sumer-producer relations. Such a signal might improve
relations between the United States and important foreign
oil suppliers.

Efforts have been made in the past to "lease" unused production from Saudi Arabia at prices below the fair market
value for the oil to be put in cheaper storage in the United
States. These initiatives were rejected by Saudi Arabian
officials who did not want to produce the resources and "lease"
them for nominal amounts such as $2 a barrel. A plan that
provided funds for the United States to pay "fair" market value
to acquire unused Saudi or other producer-country oil for
the SPR in times of market weakness would highlight the
commitment of the United States to reciprocal relations, potentially easing tensions regarding conflicting oil price goals.

b. *Establish professional criteria for managing the SPR.* A significant amount of controversy arose last year concerning President Bill Clinton's use of his discretionary authority to
lease oil to the market on a time-swap or exchange basis in
order to address winter heating-oil inventory concerns. The
criticism was threefold: (1) the exchanges reduced the size
of the SPR, making less prompt oil available to manage a
future disruption; (2) the SPR should not be used as a buffer
stock but rather to manage severe accidents or supply emergencies; and (3) the time-swap was badly managed, thus earn-

ing the government far less in interest than it should have. Unfortunately, perhaps, the government's use of its swap authority in the autumn of 2000 became associated with a policy that appeared to advocate that the SPR should be used as a market buffer stock to damp prices and price volatility. In reality, proactive use of the swap or exchange authority actually provides the government with an ability to build the SPR over time and to improve its quality through prudent use of market structures. It also enables the government to monetize its crude oil reserves, which otherwise sit idly and unproductively. The government should look into ways to improve management of the SPR through the following types of actions:

- Take advantage of the market's forward price structure to make sure the strategic reserve is strengthened efficiently over time. Thus, if the market structure were backwardated, with future prices lower than current prices, the government would be able to replenish the reserve with more oil than it had leased on an auction basis. If the market structure were in contango, with future prices higher than prompt prices, the government could lease its cheaper spare storage capacity to industry, thereby also providing revenue to build government-owned reserves at a later time. (Leasing spare tankage should also be considered separately by the Department of Defense.) If a government agency did this on a regular basis, as a standard operating procedure, it would earn far more than it did in its initial efforts in the fall of 2000 and would have a means to finance a larger reserve.

There are two objections that can be raised to this, however. First, there are potential physical limits to using underground natural salt caverns (salt domes) for storage in this manner without the need to leach them anew. Second, there are objections—as there were in 2000—on the ground that using the SPR oil in this manner reduces theoretically the amount of oil available in an emergency should one occur. That is a clear trade-off to be taken into account in policymaking.

- Seek legislative authorization to expand the government's latitude in implementing SPR exchanges. Professional management of the SPR would require an expansion of the current limits on the authority of the government to undertake time-swaps of SPR crude. Current authority limits such swaps to 30 million barrels within a specified time frame, but the reserve isn't permitted to drop below 500 million barrels. The authority for time swaps could be increased by several-fold.

c. *Establish Clear Policy for Use of the SPR.* The administration should as an early priority define publicly its general policy for using SPR crude. It is especially important during times of lost supply and uncertainty about future supply for the government to damp speculation that breeds price volatility. For example, in August 1990, when Iraq invaded Kuwait, the government delayed an announcement about use of the SPR until January 1991. Had the SPR been used by September 1990, if for no other reason than to calm markets until supplies could be fully made up from other sources, the price spike of that autumn could have been reduced and the likelihood of a recession in 1991 also reduced. The administration should therefore define its position on the SPR soon. It should provide general criteria for determining when strategic stocks might be tapped under the president's authority, defining more generally what will be considered an emergency and what conditions might prompt the president to authorize a time-swap. The administration should also determine what conditions might prompt the Department of Energy to either accelerate purchases for the SPR or to lease out storage space to industry when future and forward oil price curves encourage this. Finally, the administration should improve the operability of the SPR. Unlike commercial stocks, the recent release of the SPR (mostly sweet) crude showed that the industry isn't fully educated about logistical issues involved in getting SPR oil into the domestic refining system efficiently. Therefore it would be prudent to review and highlight the negative experiences of those who participated in last year's exchange program.

It should be noted that clarification of the use of the SPR would have a couple of additional benefits. It would eliminate debate or trial balloons to media in the event of an interruption that meets the clear criteria set by policy. Trial balloons or public debate often cloud market transparency to the detriment of predictable price formation and orderly markets. Public articulation of policy would also eliminate the risk of holding hostage a release of strategic stocks to the production policy of key OPEC countries.

- Coordinate use of the SPR with other IEA countries. It goes without saying that the United States should coordinate release of the SPR in cooperation with other IEA countries. This would be especially important either in the case of a market in which one or more producer countries intentionally reduces or bans exports in order to increase prices, or in case of market disruption. Nonetheless, it should also be recognized that unilateral use of the SPR by the United States might be criticized for giving other countries that do not cooperate a "free ride" on the benefits of the SPR release. The free rider problem may well be an unavoidable consequence of having and using the SPR—otherwise the United States would have to consult and share decisions about its use, which would also be risky and questionable.

- Coordinate use of the SPR with actions by key producer countries. One of the unnoticed and less criticized aspects of the use of the SPR exchange by the United States in 2000 was that it was performed in a "cooperation" rather than a "confrontation" mode with producer countries in both OPEC and elsewhere. Only after the OPEC secretariat and key OPEC members repeatedly stated that "we have done our part" in easing the market and that "it is up to the industrialized countries to do their part," was the SPR exchange actually triggered. Its timing demonstrated that in a cooperative mode, use of the SPR could work hand-in-hand with diplomacy vis-à-vis producing nations. (See next section, number 4, below.)

d. *Review tax, accounting, and other factors affecting industry's incentives to hold petroleum product and natural gas inventories, with the intent of enhancing inventories before seasonal demand and neutralizing any adverse impact of current rules.*

There has been significant bipartisan support in oil "consuming" areas of the United States for government-controlled stockpiles of products and even of critical product components (e.g., ethanol). There has also been support for state governments' mandating minimum stocks for fuel-switching purposes of certain categories of consumers, including power plants. The federal government last year also established the Northeast Heating Oil Reserve. Given the critical role played by inventories in smoothing out supply shortfalls, the government should undertake a wholesale review of product inventories and consider incentives to industry to hold higher levels of inventory than has recently been the case.

Industry inventories would be an alternative to the federal Northeast Heating Oil Reserve. Industry generally fails to build inventory when futures markets are in backwardation; that is, when futures prices are lower than prompt prices. Industry builds stocks when markets are in contango and industry expects that future prices will be higher than prompt prices. Since industry is now managing inventories on a just-in-time basis, there is a danger that market structure will not go sufficiently into contango when product builds are required. Therefore, industry will not have an incentive to build gasoline stocks in advance of the traditional summer driving season or heating oil and natural gas stocks in advance of the traditional winter heating seasons. An alternative incentive could come from fiscal measures that reward firms that carry seasonal inventory or penalize firms that do not.

Accounting rules, especially "last-in, first-out" (LIFO) rules, create year-end changes in inventory in order for companies to reduce their tax liabilities. The federal government should review national and state government rules and their impacts on corporate inventory management positions, with the intent of neutralizing any incentive on the part of companies to reduce stocks at year-end when markets do not require rapid de-stocking.

e. *Encourage states to review minimum inventory for fuel switching where feasible and also fiscal incentives to industry to build inventories in advance of seasonal demand increases.* Such an effort could be incorporated into incentive programs for state governments cooperating with one another on a regional basis. (See recommendations for immediate actions, above.) States have traditionally made the issue of backup supplies part of their regulatory frameworks. These requirements have generally faded in the age of deregulation and should be reexamined.

4. Develop Mechanisms for a New National Approach to Energy Policy

If the energy policy goals of the country are to be articulated coherently and implemented effectively, steps need to be taken to build as wide a consensus politically as possible, especially if the tradeoffs among conflicting internal objectives of policy are to be successfully worked out. This means that constituencies must be brought together at several levels: within the federal government administration, between the administration and Congress, between the federal government and state governments, and between the federal government and the public at large. In order to further this end, a series of steps should be considered:

a. *Create an appropriate interagency process to articulate and promote energy security policy and integrate energy policy with overall economic, environmental, and foreign policy.* For energy policy to be integrated with overall economic policy, environmental policy, and foreign policy, it needs to be vetted and articulated through a "permanent" interagency process that brings those responsible for these areas together. The Bush administration has moved rapidly in this direction through the creation of the White House Energy Policy Development Group headed by Vice President Dick Cheney. That group appropriately includes representatives from the Departments of Energy, Interior, Commerce, Treasury, and State as well as from the Environmental Protection Agency and the Federal Emergency Management Agency (FEMA). As this process unfolds, the administration should find ways to establish a permanent framework for articulating energy policy, perhaps including representation from the Department of Defense as well. The secretary of energy should then be empowered to carry forward and implement the policy recommendations of the Policy Development Group.

b. *Review and streamline the allocation of authorities within the federal government, especially in areas of land management and energy.* The federal government has been institutionally hampered in its ability to articulate and implement a coherent national energy policy by the allocation of disparate and overlapping authorities across government departments. For example, the fact that land management for resource exploitation is managed by the Department of the Interior rather than the Department of Energy has created inefficiency in government decision-making that should be reevaluated. The White House Energy Policy Development Group should, in the process of its work, review such discrepancies in authority and make recommendations for streamlining them.

c. *Convene a National Energy Summit to help develop a national consensus on energy policy objectives and means.* The administration should use whatever mechanisms are at its disposal to educate the public concerning its views on how the nation's energy problems can be dealt with. It should use similar mechanisms to forge the kind of domestic consensus that is likely to be required if its energy policy goals are to be implemented. One possible way to do this is by convening a nonpartisan, multi-industry summit, possibly chaired by the vice president, to review its national energy plan as developed by the Energy Policy Development Group. The summit should be designed not only to vet energy proposals to as wide a group of responsible companies and institutionalized interest groups as possible, but also to elicit proposals from those represented.

d. *Develop a Strategic Communications Plan on Energy Security Policy in order to educate the public on the difficulties of achieving short-term, unilateral solutions to the nation's energy dilemmas.* The administration should conduct a thorough survey of constituency and advocacy groups within the country in order to develop initiatives concerning ways to build a national consensus on energy policy. It should unfold a strategic communications plan with the goal of gaining support of environmental groups and congressional leadership on whatever tradeoffs may be involved in its energy policy. For example, it should indicate its resolve to produce cleaner fuels if in its judgment it is also recommending temporary delays in new restrictions (such as sulfur production) or other environmental goals for compelling economic and national security requirements.

LONG-TERM POLICY INITIATIVES

1. Review International Approaches to Build, Maintain, and Use Strategic and Commercial Crude Oil and Petroleum Product Inventories

The administration should, in parallel with a review of our national approach to strategic and commercial petroleum and petroleum product inventories, conduct a review of other approaches both in the International Energy Agency and by non-IEA members. The United States needs to work together with other oil consuming and importing countries to assure that there are adequate strategic stockpiles available globally to manage future disruptions, beginning with a new definition of "adequate." Two significant problems need to be reviewed and dealt with:

- First, the entire structure for managing supply disruptions is built around the notion that physical shortfalls can be measured independent of prices and in volumetric terms alone. The assumption that release of global strategic stocks could be triggered by a volumetric shortfall that was to be coordinated by an oil supply-sharing facility is outdated. It was predicated on a world of regulated trade flows that disappeared with market deregulation in the 1970s and 1980s. Instead, planning needs to be based on today's fast-paced global market and on the sorts of disruptions that are most apt to face us now, rather than those that were most likely in 1975.
- Second, the mechanisms for dealing with disruptions are built almost exclusively within the institution and membership of the IEA. IEA or OECD countries dominated global oil trade when the IEA was founded in 1974. Today its share is rapidly falling. Between 1985 and 2000, East Asian countries alone increased their share of global oil consumption from less than 20 percent to more than 27 percent, as the region represented 80 percent of the total increase in worldwide demand. As IEA oil use continues to stagnate and as developing countries increase their individual oil consumption and share of global consumption, mechanisms need to be developed to encourage these high-demand growth countries to build their own strategic stockpiles. They also need to participate in the global planning that occurs within the IEA.

a. *Enhance and modernize IEA strategic stockpile policies in light of the changed international market, taking into account situations that technically fall short of a supply disruption as well as different regulatory authorities among IEA members.*

The IEA should initiate a strategic review related to the size of strategic stockpiles as well as their management. The review should recognize that the divergent approaches taken within the organization to strategic stock management make harmonization difficult. This is especially true for the relationship between the European Union, with its requirement that refiners should hold stocks related to seventy-five days of consumption (sixty-five days for non-refiners) and the IEA, with its requirement that countries cover ninety days of net imports. It should also try to find ways to harmonize the differences that exist between those countries that hold government strategic stocks (essentially the United States, Germany, and to some degree Japan) and the others, which require inventories be held by companies.

Harmonization of plans within the IEA needs to take into account the following issues, among others:

1. Situations requiring international coordination of stock release, short of a full supply disruption.

2. The differences between those that hold crude oil stocks and those that hold products, given the fact that release into the market of crude oil supplies affects markets indirectly, while release into the market of products affects markets directly and immediately.

3. Differences between those with authority to use strategic oil on an exchange basis (essentially only the United States) and those permitted to use it only in an emergency. Efforts should be made to harmonize authorities in case decisions are made to release stocks in situations not covered by a shortfall that is fully defined as a supply disruption.

b. *Encourage key non-IEA countries (e.g., China, India, Brazil) to develop strategic stocks.*

The International Energy Agency was created a quarter of a century ago as a mutual-protection society of OECD countries. Designed as a political grouping to prevent any oil-producing countries from using oil exports as a political instrument to influence the foreign policies of IEA members, the IEA was formed at a time when the OECD countries dominated global energy consumption. Today it excludes the most rapidly growing energy-consuming countries in the world—China, India, and Brazil among them.

And, as a result, these new consumers become vulnerable economically in times of disruptions as well as vulnerable potentially to political pressures of producers.

Part of the problem relates to free-riding. Countries that do not belong to the IEA can and do free-ride at present. Any country that releases stocks or undertakes policies to reduce its exposure to price shocks will bear the costs of that action but the benefits accrue to all consumers including the large consuming countries that are not members, such as China, India, Pakistan, and Brazil. But part of the problem relates to what countries with rapidly growing oil demand and imports should do for their own economic well-being and to prevent spillover of economic problems they might encounter to the large industrial countries. Moreover, at present some IEA members, Japan in particular, are working bilaterally with neighboring states to do this.

c. *Review IEA membership, taking into account the desirability of creating a new class of associated members who could be encouraged to hold minimum stocks and also benefit from direct participation in other IEA activities.*

Although informal programs to encourage stocking by developing world countries would have a positive impact, such efforts cannot replace the more effective tool of centralized coordination with the IEA. Centralized efforts are needed so that international norms and standards can be met during a crisis. This would be the case even if Japan opts to finance such stocking activities by Asian countries on its own. The United States should initiate a review of ways the IEA can work with key countries that are not members of the IEA to encourage them to define their strategic oil stockpile requirements and to build strategic stocks (or to create minimum inventory requirements for industry). The IEA should also consider creating a new class of associated members who, in exchange for making commitments to hold minimum stocks, would gain direct benefit from participating in certain IEA activities.

2. Accelerate Demand-Management Efforts at Home and Internationally

The United States has trailed other industrialized societies when it comes to oil-demand management. Most other industrialized countries have used fiscal policy to curb the growth in oil demand by heavily taxing petroleum products. While those efforts can be criticized on numerous grounds—as they have been by oil-producing countries—there is little doubt about their effectiveness in limiting the exposure of the economy to oil price shocks and promoting energy efficiency and conservation. Still, it remains the case in the United States that demand management has in recent years been the rhetorical stepchild of national energy policy, even with the implementation of Corporate Average Fuel Economy (CAFE) standards, appliance standards, and tax credits for a range of investments.

Yet it is clear that active demand-management policies could have less expensive and equally large impacts on the balance between supply and demand as supply-side solutions. Moreover, it is almost certainly the case that any supply-side efforts will need to be joined with vigorous demand-management actions to gain congressional approval as an overall energy legislative package.

The government should recognize that it has significant impacts on demand through its regulatory, tax, and incentives framework. It also has a considerable ability to remove distortions in regulations and to promote market flexibility, with an eye on the impact of its actions on demand management. With 60 percent of U.S. oil consumption focused on transportation, the administration should encourage industry and government investments in technologies to increase the fuel efficiency of the nation's fleet and to stimulate domestic development and deployment of fuel-efficient vehicles, including gasoline/electric or fuel cell hybrids. Actions could include the following:

    a. *Take a proactive government position on demand management.* The best way to capture the nation's attention on demand management is for the president to take leadership in mapping out a demand-management program as part of the nation's energy strategy. Follow-up positions and speeches by the vice president and secretary of energy could specify the levels of supply savings that are targeted. They should also specify how these targets can be reached and how demand management can impact them (for example, with respect to sectors like transportation, residential, commercial, industrial, and power, and with respect to choice of fuels such as clean coal, cleaner oil, gas, nuclear, renewable sources, and new technologies).

b. *Use federal procurement authority to enhance use of alternative fuels and develop programs to introduce new efficiency technologies into federal buildings and nascent transportation technologies into government vehicle fleets.* The federal government has an enormous impact on fuel choices in the market through its procurement policies. These policies should be used to invest in alternative fuels, including ethanol, natural gas and hydrogen, or hybrid vehicles, and they should incentivize the development of alternative fuel infrastructures. For example, under most current programs, federal and state agencies have been purchasing vehicles with flexible fuel use rather than vehicles mandated to actually use alternative fuels in question or emerging technology that greatly improves mileage standards. The result has been the perpetuation of gasoline use and traditional engines rather than use of alternative fuels or engine designs. This squanders both the demonstration impact of federal programs as well as the opportunity to create infrastructures for supply and fueling alternative design vehicles.

It should be said, however, that the purchase of alternative design vehicles could be more expensive than conventional vehicles and might encumber unanticipated repair problems. There are clear cautions to worry about. Efforts to mandate dual-fired ethanol cars, for example, to fulfill the alternative vehicle mandates of the Energy Policy Conservation Act, were little more than bones to domestic interest groups rather than scientific efforts at promoting alternative fuels. It is also the case that federal purchasing of a particular design solution or fuel puts the federal government in the business of trying to anticipate future market preferences and benefits. These objections need to be taken into account in designing the federal government's strategy. But they need not stop the efforts as outlined. These efforts should be viewed as an investment that promotes options of significance for energy security.

c. *Use federal procurement authority to achieve other demand management goals.* For example, review and rigorously implement minimal targets for mileage standards for the federal automotive fleet, standards for energy conservation in federal buildings, and other current standards already in effect.

d. *Review and establish new and stricter CAFE mileage standards, especially for light trucks.* There are many good reasons to accelerate efforts to reclassify SUVs and other vehicles (currently classified as "trucks") as "automobiles," for the purposes of application of CAFE as well as emissions standards. For example, mandating CAFE minimum fuel-mileage standards for light trucks of 25 miles per gallon (comparable level to four-door automobiles) could save 925,000 b/d of fuel demand. While the automotive industry has traditionally argued that artificial standards can weaken its profitability and therefore its ability to maintain employment levels and investments in competitive vehicles, it is also the case that such standards can increase the industry's longer-term global competitive position given other suppliers' efforts in this direction. It must be noted, however, that it takes seven to ten years for the entire U.S. automobile fleet to turn over. Therefore, changes to CAFE standards are not likely to have instantaneous results, which is a good reason to start now. Some tax breaks to consumers who purchase cars with more favorable mileage could hasten the process of moving low-mileage cars off the road quickly. Even without government intervention, hybrid vehicles still could make up as much as 15–20 percent of new vehicle purchases, experts predict. This will contribute to a drop in U.S. oil demand of 600,000 b/d. Studies show that tax incentives can hasten and magnify this process.

e. *Actively promote the development of energy efficient technologies, including fuel-efficient engine and vehicle technologies* to encourage more efficient worldwide use of scarce oil resources. China alone is projected to add more than 150 million automobiles to the road in the next two decades. Efficiency of that fleet has global implications for oil requirements.

3. Maximize Efforts to Develop Clean Sources of Domestic Fuel Supply

There is no doubt that the United States has a premier energy resource base. But it is a mature province whose potential exceeds that of many other conventional resource provinces. In addition, it is physically incapable of rendering this country energy independent given our extremely high energy consumption rates. And, during the past twenty years, while other countries have made more of their resource base available for energy resource exploration and exploitation, the United States is virtually unique in removing significant acreage that was once available for these purposes from energy development.

The United States requires a better-balanced and more integrated approach to maintenance and enhancement of the environment and energy-supply objectives. Twenty years ago, nearly 75 percent of federal lands were available for private lease to oil and gas exploration companies. Since then the share has fallen to about 17 percent. And a significant share of the remaining 17 percent is for all practical purposes unavailable for drilling.

The Bush administration made vocal campaign promises about one major potential oil and gas province—the coastal plain of the Arctic National Wildlife Refuge. (It also supports a pipeline to bring some 49 trillion cubic feet of Prudhoe Bay gas reserves to the lower forty-eight states, a proposal that is designed to expand opportunities for additional gas exploration in Alaska.) As the Task Force prepares its proposals, it cautions that unless the administration's proposals to permit exploration in the ANWR take into account other aspects of policy—including other aspects of land management as well as environmental policy and demand-management policy—the administration could seriously erode support for its ANWR proposals.

The Task Force recommends consideration of the following with respect to domestic resources and energy use. These recommendations recognize that at present domestic drilling is constrained by many factors other than availability of land. They also recognize that sound energy policy must begin at home since, from three perspectives, it is desirable to foster domestic supply: national security, balance of payments, and the comparative advantage of American industry. Even so, lack of equipment and personnel, in particular, will curtail the expansion of domestic and international supplies for a number of years.

a. *Oil and Natural Gas*

1. Accelerate completion of the U.S. oil and gas reserve inventory, as mandated by Congress, highlighting restrictions on resource development. Such an inventory needs to be completed soon and well before any plan is adopted to develop particular domestic resources. The secretary of the interior has been mandated to conduct an inventory of all onshore federal lands, identifying reserve estimates as well as restrictions on resource development on them. It is critical that this inventory be completed soon and well before any plan is adopted to develop particular domestic resources. It could well turn out, for example, that the estimated 300 trillion cubic feet of natural gas resources in the Rocky Mountain Overthrust could be a more appropriate and cost-effective target for industry exploitation than the distant resources of the ANWR. The virtues of completing the inventory first are that it would provide an information base on which intelligent decision-making concerning land availability can be made. It would also provide a more scientific base for any tradeoffs than need to be accommodated with conflicting environmental and other land-use policies. Additionally, expanding this national effort to an international one that

includes Canada and Mexico as well could be an important step in delineating a hemispheric energy policy.

2.　　Undertake an accelerated and complete review of tax
and fiscal policy as they impact oil and gas development
in the United States, taking into account the competitive position of the U.S. fiscal regime as compared to
international conditions, in order to attract more capital
to the sector. While the United States has a mature oil
and gas resource base, it also has one of the least efficient
tax regimes in the world when it comes to oil and gas development. The main direct tax is the royalty—which has
a well-understood negative impact on development and
field abandonment. Changes to federal corporate taxes,
especially during the 1980s, further exposed the oil and
gas industry. The Alternative Minimum Tax has also
posed a major problem to development of supply in that
it deters activity in a cyclical downturn. Industry has
been adverse to a tax review—except with respect to
royalty holidays—because of fear that it could lead to even
more restrictive policies (especially during a period when
the exploration and production sector is reaping record
taxes). Yet any effort to enhance domestic supply must
be based on what makes for sensible fiscal incentives.
The administration should be encouraged, therefore, to
undertake this fiscal review as it also reviews its land
management policies.

b. *Electricity*

1.　　Create an appropriate comprehensive statutory framework for electricity restructuring and for reestablishing
a capacity cushion for the nation's power supplies. A
new framework needs to overcome the adverse impacts
of today's highly fragmented regime, which has reduced
the reliability of the U.S. power grid and impeded investment in new generation and transmission capacity. This
is a key conclusion highlighted by the regional and
national impacts of the California power crisis on elec-

tricity supplies and the economy. The patchwork nature of twenty-five separate state legal and regulatory frameworks has reduced the reliability of the transmission network and impeded investment in new generation and transmission capacity as these jurisdictions have instituted some form of electricity deregulation or restructuring. The uneven landscape of state-by-state deregulation, and growing competition for power supplies between regions, have produced a climate of investment uncertainty that is inhibiting system upgrades and expansion at a time of dramatically increasing electricity demand. Thus, states must work together with each other and with the federal government to ensure that regional power and transmission markets are efficient and competitive. State and federal authorities must also provide for the continued reliability of the interstate bulk power grid. The challenge will be simultaneously to do the following: meet increased demand for reliable and high-quality electric power; create a favorable investment climate to expand the power infrastructure to meet demand; expedite the development of new infrastructure; increase the efficiency of power generation and distribution; and, at the same time, mitigate the ongoing impacts of power generation, distribution, and use on the environment.

2.   Work expeditiously to improve the statutory framework for approvals of the siting of power generating plants, as well as transmission and distribution infrastructure. This is likely to require an unprecedented level of cooperation between the federal, state, and local governments, as well as environmental, consumer, and industry stakeholders. Only the federal administration can provide the focus and leadership such an effort requires. The administration thus needs to consider incentives to states and localities to work together to encourage rapid construction of the required infrastructure.

3.   Evaluate the need for incentives to stimulate the introduction of new technologies into the power market-

place, including distributed generation and co-generation. Working with industry partners, the administration should work to substantially increase investment in technologies that enhance the efficiency, reliability, and quality of the power transmission and distribution infrastructure. Policy should also focus on reducing the business, regulatory, legal, technological, and institutional barriers to the market introduction of new electricity technologies, such as distributed generation and co-generation. And the administration should continue to promote research and development for alternative sources of power and work with industry to help stimulate deployment of these technologies.

4. Work with state regulators and regional authorities to allow and incentivize companies to offer long-term contracts for electric power and to encourage them to hedge price risks associated with such contracts to maximize the part of the market that will not be susceptible to large shifts in the spot market price. The use of long-term contracts should help protect consumers from wild swings in electricity rates when a shortage occurs in markets. The downside is that companies that are not successfully hedged can be forced into bankruptcy by the margin call on adverse market swings or by an unwise hedging program. Experience shows that even the most expert traders can make these errors. Thus, the institution of long-term contracting is only a partial solution.

5. Encourage the development of power capacity cushions on a regional basis. For example, it could consider providing incentives to system operators to buy stand-by power at auction to cover anticipated energy level needs, in order to encourage construction and maintenance of spare capacity. The guaranteed market and forward sale of stand-by power will encourage generators to build up incremental capacity and to maintain spare generation capacity that can be used to smooth out market disruptions or anomalies. Although this will mean that overall costs for

electricity might be slightly higher on a long-term basis, it will prevent sudden sharp rises that can be harmful to the public good.

6.   Recognize that many of the policies and actions that are needed to meet increased demand for power generation are power source-specific.

7.   Assure that regulations protect open access to electricity generated by new, nontraditional fuel sources. This action is necessary to guarantee that new sources cannot be locked out of the transmission system by suppliers using traditional fuels.

c. *Natural Gas*

1.   Apply strong leadership to develop a coherent, comprehensive strategy promoting efficient development and use of the nation's natural gas resources. National policy can be especially effective in enhancing market efficiencies and in accelerating long-term supply. This was the conclusion of the National Petroleum Council's December 1999 report on "Natural Gas: Meeting the Challenge of the Nation's Growing Natural Gas Demand." There is no doubt that a strong White House role is required to coordinate the array of disparate government departments and independent federal agencies that play a part in decision-making on natural gas. A strong White House role is also required to promote collaboration between federal, state, local, and tribal governments, in order to ensure the availability and deliverability of natural gas to all classes of consumers.

2.   Endorse the construction of natural gas pipelines from the Arctic to the lower forty-eight states and work bilaterally with Canada and the state of Alaska to address important issues that need to be resolved. U.S.-Canadian relations are critical for delivering natural gas to the lower forty-eight. Without full cooperation from Canada, efforts to harness additional resources from Alaska will be stymied. Critical support for the pipeline would

include making the infrastructure permitting process efficient and helping resolve differences surrounding questions of routing, environment, and construction. This calls for a federal role in coordinating authorities in Alaska, within a variety of U.S. federal agencies, and with Canada.

3. Assure that regulatory authorities work together to bring about natural gas market efficiencies, including the provision of open access to markets by producers and to supply by end users, and that allow delivery costs to be determined transparently by market forces so that commodity values are transparent to both producers and consumers. The regulatory process needs to ensure that delivery systems provide open access to markets by producers and to supply by end users. Regulators should promote efficiencies that allow delivery costs to be determined by market forces so that commodity values are transparent to both producers and consumers. Regulations also need to protect open access to electricity generated by new fuels outside the traditional domain, such as fuel cells or biomass. This means that regulators should:

- Carry out regular pipeline rate reviews to assure that cost reductions are passed along to consumers.
- Promote incentive rate-making plans to tie the financial returns of pipelines to efficiency gains and losses. Such plans should also require sharing of efficiency gains with customers.

4. Invest in—or stimulate and encourage private-sector investment in—research and development of technologies that focus on safe and cost-effective ultra-deep water production, smaller drilling footprints, and increased production from nonconventional sources, including methane hydrates. Production of abundant and affordable gas supply in environmentally sensitive ways will depend on technology developments.

5. Encourage natural gas exploration and production through a series of technology-targeted tax incentives that

also encourage use of advanced, environmentally sensitive technologies and that provide counter-cyclical support for exploration and production (e.g., geological and geophysical expensing, deepwater, marginal gas well production, and infrastructure investments in such equipment as drilling rigs).

6. Initiate a mitigation forum process to evaluate infrastructure needs and reduce delays in new pipelines and storage facility siting. The process should involve regulators, environmentalists, technology developers, landowners, consumer advocates, and industry users. In this manner authorization to construct new pipeline infrastructure should be accomplished without undue delay, consistent with ensuring that environmental factors are fully considered and addressed. This new infrastructure will be needed to meet growing demand and to relieve capacity constraints wherever they exist. The federal government should work with industry and state agencies to re-engineer underground storage facilities.

7. Consider providing incentives to state and local governments that agree to expedite natural gas infrastructure siting.

8. Invest in—or stimulate and encourage private sector investment in—technologies to ensure pipeline infrastructure integrity, reliability, flexibility, and safety.

9. Foster development of advanced storage technologies to increase regional storage capacity and serve peak power and distributed generation markets.

10. Evaluate the potential of imported liquefied natural gas as a major additional source of base load as well as incremental supply for the United States, and in the process consider accelerating environmental reviews required for siting as well as accommodating the commercial logistics and other user needs associated with facilities built or operated by LNG suppliers. Accommodation of the commercial logistics and needs associated with LNG

regasification facilities will be important where such facilities may be built or operated by LNG suppliers. Government policy will need to address means of accommodating the commercial practicalities that attend supplier-driven LNG facilities.

d. *Coal*

Given the nation's abundance of coal resources, it is critical to foster the development of clean coal technologies such as gasification to promote coal use in power generation. At the same time, such development programs should mitigate the environmental impacts of coal combustion to meet local, regional, and global environmental challenges. Coal use continues to grow—it currently supplies 55 percent of U.S. power generation and has increased in absolute volume by 17 percent in the last decade. Its abundance makes it a fuel of choice for national energy security reasons; but its use poses some of the most difficult environmental challenges of energy production. Its worldwide use is also expected to grow dramatically, as it represents an abundant and inexpensive source of fuel for power in numerous fast-growing developing countries, including China and India.

Investment in clean coal technologies continues to pay dividends. For example, in the United States, increased coal use has been accompanied by reduced sulfur emissions. These proven technologies need to be deployed more broadly and further advances in them need to be promoted through a renewed focus on research and development, as well as fiscal incentives that are offered to these ends. The government needs also to find ways to foster entirely new technologies, such as carbon sequestration technologies that could dramatically increase the attraction of coal internationally as a fuel whose use would not generate large greenhouse-gas emissions.

The vital importance of further breakthroughs in the area of clean coal cannot be understated. It could be a major contribution to U.S. and global solutions to energy and environmental needs.

e. *Nuclear*

1. Support the Nuclear Regulatory Commission in relicensing expeditiously plants whose licenses will soon expire in order to extend plant life where possible. Nuclear power plants now generate about 20 percent of the country's power. Existing plants are operating with unprecedented capacity factors of more than 85 percent. The importance of this significant base load has been reinforced by recent events in California. Increased attention to power plant emissions, especially greenhouse gases, may further increase the attractiveness of nuclear power. Licenses of operating plants, some initially granted for forty years, are beginning to expire in 2010. The NRC is beginning to relicense to extend plant life by an additional twenty years.

2. Work constructively with stakeholders to resolve nuclear power plant spent fuel (and high-level defense waste) disposition within the next few years, since this is critical to preserving viable nuclear options for the nation. This will require high-level administration attention. In particular, the scientific study of Yucca Mountain as a repository site and parallel development of engineered barriers will present the president and Congress with the final suitability decision and licensing application in about a year. If the site is deemed suitable based on science and technology, the administration should work with the state of Nevada, the nuclear utilities, and the stakeholders to develop a path forward to resolve current disputes and meet federal responsibilities of accepting spent fuel, as well as disposing of high-level defense waste.

3. Work to improve the investment climate for new nuclear power plant construction, through NRC streamlining of licensing procedures and by resolving uncertainties surrounding electricity deregulation and restructuring. No

new nuclear power plants have been ordered in the United States for more than twenty years. But the impact of reactor accidents at Three Mile Island and Chernobyl may well be fading, with the excellent safety record of Western-designed reactors and the availability of more advanced designs and their additional safety features. However, safety alone is not the issue. Uncertainty surrounding deregulation is also a problem, given the very large capital costs of nuclear plants.

4.   Work with Congress to sustain the front-end domestic nuclear fuel cycle through the next half-decade. A key element is the development of U.S.-origin competitive enrichment technology. The front-end of the nuclear fuel cycle requires attention. Congress has established a statutory requirement to maintain viable domestic uranium mining, conversion, and enrichment industries, yet all three sectors are unhealthy. Uranium enrichment is particularly sensitive because of its implications for nuclear weapons proliferation, and reliability of American enrichment supply is as important for slowing the spread of enrichment technology as it is for supplying domestic utilities.

5.   Work with Western European allies and Japan to shape a future nuclear fuel cycle that would garner shared support. The very large disconnect between U.S. versus European and Japanese fuel-cycle policies is detrimental to sustaining nuclear power as a viable and potentially important option. Unresolved issues concerning spent-fuel isolation plague the choice of an open fuel cycle by the United States (i.e., once-through utilization of nuclear fuel followed by geological disposal). The alternative closed fuel cycle advanced by France, Japan, and others (i.e., reprocessing spent fuel to extract and recycle plutonium) is plagued by large accumulation of separated plutonium and unfavorable economics. The proliferation danger posed by separated plutonium led to the U.S. decision in the 1970s to pursue the open fuel cycle. The administration needs to work actively and closely with allies to

help shape a future fuel cycle that would satisfy our non-proliferation concerns and their energy security needs, while minimizing waste issues and enhancing safety.

6.   Work with the education system to reinvigorate training in nuclear science and technology. There has been a precipitous drop in the number of American students studying nuclear engineering, and some leading universities are on the threshold of irrevocably cutting out the relevant essential educational programs and infrastructures. The administration needs to work with the university community to sustain nuclear science and technology education during the next decade in order to help preserve the nuclear power option. New technologies such as small innovative reactors promise to offer an alternative to traditional designs and the problems described above.

4. Augment Diplomatic Initiatives to Spur Non-OPEC Production Increases

The more supply that is available on international energy markets and the more diversified its sources, the better equipped markets will be to handle a disruption without a market failure or extreme price response. The United States has a stated policy favoring diversity of oil supply and working to promote oil production from countries outside of OPEC.

a. *Expand Oil and Gas Forum programs*

One method used to promote investment in non-OPEC resources and to remove fiscal, bureaucratic, or political obstacles thwarting such investment is to convene major trade conclaves involving U.S. energy companies and political leaders from non-OPEC countries. The Departments of Energy, Commerce, and State together have initiated such forums as the China Oil and Gas Forum and the Latin American Oil and Gas Forum, which provide a venue for discussion of investment opportunities and problems among U.S. industry, U.S. government, and non-OPEC industry and government. The budget for such programs should be expanded to cover other important oil-producing countries or regions such as Russia, West Africa, the Caspian, and Indonesia.

b. *Investigate ways to facilitate increased investment in Mexico's oil and gas sectors*

Mexico is one of the four largest oil suppliers to the United States and could become a significant natural gas producer if it had the resources to finance additional exploration activities in the Yucatan peninsula. Northern Mexico has strong demand for natural gas and electric power and currently imports a net of 0.25 billion cubic meters of natural gas from the United States. Mexico has an important role to play in North American energy markets, and assistance should be brought to bear in its struggle to finance a higher level of investment in its hydrocarbons sector. Higher production of natural gas in Mexico would not only satisfy demand from northern Mexico, creating a backup for natural gas supply in the United States, but could be an important source to meet rising U.S. demand. At a minimum, the administration should investigate ways to support Mexican government investment in natural gas resources. But the administration may also want to consider leverage tools that could be brought to bear to assist political leaders in Mexico who advocate that Mexico open its energy sector to foreign investment, starting with natural gas. This latter policy would garner the strong support of U.S. energy companies and demonstrate the administration's commitment to increase natural gas supplies in the hemisphere. Activity that would encourage U.S. participation in Mexico's energy industry would deflect suggestions that support for Mexico's oil and gas industry should take a second seat to developing U.S.-based resources.

Ultimately, Mexico's resources are closer and maybe more economical to develop than those in Alaska. However, Mexico's constitution blocks ownership participation in oil and gas fields by foreign entities, and Mexico's oil workers unions are heavily set against any foreign participation in Mexico's oil and gas activities under any kind of arrangement. Thus,

U.S. visibility on this issue could create some political tension with Mexico in the short term, even if it is beneficial for both countries in the longer term. One solution to this dilemma might be to keep discussion of opening Mexico's natural gas sector within a hemispheric focus, including Canadian and Brazilian oil and gas firms as well as American firms, in order to diffuse attention from the negative aspects of Mexican popular opinion regarding U.S.-led investment in Mexican resources.

c. *Encourage reforms in Russia's energy sector*

Further enhancement of the Russian energy sector would help the United States attain the diverse oil and gas supplies that will be needed during the coming years to moderate rising dependence on the Middle East. Without a massive injection of capital, Russia's production, which has dropped by half since the collapse of the Soviet Union, could continue to stagnate if not fall in the coming years. Russian oil production is projected to rise only marginally to about 6.5 million b/d during the next decade and then only if investments can be increased to twice the current level, according to Russia's Ministry for Fuel and Energy. Investment scandals, poorly articulated property rights, unstable tax and legal regimes, and bureaucratic barriers have had a chilling effect on foreign investment, scaring away most international investors from Russia's energy sector. The Gore-Chernomerdyn effort included a rehabilitation package for Russia's oil and gas industry but many of the funds allocated were not extended due to the significant barriers encountered by U.S. companies trying to operate in the country.

However, there appears to be a major change taking place in Russia under President Vladimir Putin, whose government is showing renewed interest in energy-sector reform, and new oil and gas laws look to be forthcoming. This progress from the Russian side might open the door for a new initiative from the United States on energy trade and investment, as well as the development of a production-sharing agreement law. In particular, the United States should support European initiatives to bring Russia into the European energy charter. (See section on multilateral institutions, recommendations 7 and 9.) However, while energy is a potential area of cooperation between the United States and Russia, other foreign policy and security issues are likely to take precedence. Still, the United States must consider seriously the fact that a declining Russian energy industry, while possibly curbing Russia's military budget and thereby reducing Moscow's ability to challenge U.S. interests, will make it extremely difficult for the United States to promote diversity of international supply. Given Russia's important role as an energy supplier to Europe, U.S.-Russia policy should not be pursued without debate concerning energy supply considerations and consequences.

d. *Improve access to information, as well as transparency of comparative oil and gas fiscal commercial regimes*

Oil and gas investment in any particular country or region is influenced not only by geology, but also by the fiscal regime and other aspects of government take. Experience has shown that major changes in tax policy can stimulate new investment and delay a decline in oil production or even promote a production increase in mature fields. This was clearly demonstrated through the 1980s in the U.K. sector of the North Sea. Non-OPEC countries must stay abreast of international trends in fiscal terms and other aspects of government take to ensure that their investment terms remain competitive; but competitors may seek to cloud transparency for competitive reasons, making it difficult for countries to know when an improvement in terms is necessary. The United States has a strong interest in promoting transparency and education about trends in oil and gas investment terms in non-OPEC to help keep these countries competitive and attractive for investors. This can be handled via the Oil and Gas Forums mentioned above, through reviving the program of publicly available embassy reports on the oil and gas industries of various host countries, and through U.S. Agency for International Development (AID)-sponsored training programs, as well as through Internet resources such as the Department of Energy website and IEA reports.

5. Initiate Diplomatic Efforts to Spur the Reopening of Countries That Have Nationalized and Monopolized Their Upstream Sectors

Middle East Gulf crude oil currently makes up around 25 percent of world oil supply, but could rise to 30–40 percent during the next decade as the region's key producers pursue higher investments to capture expanding demand for oil in Asia and the developing world. If political factors were to block the development of new oil fields in the Gulf, the ramifications for world oil markets could be quite severe.

There have been discussions in several important oil producing countries, notably Saudi Arabia and Kuwait, to reopen their upstream oil and gas sectors to foreign investors to garner the necessary finance and technology for the massive investment necessary—estimated at anywhere from $6 to $40 billion. This reopening is important and should be on the bilateral U.S. agenda with these countries. The Department of State, together with the National Security Council, the Department of Energy, and the Department of Commerce, should develop a strategic plan to encourage reopening to foreign investment in these important states of the Middle East Gulf. While there is no question that this investment is vitally important to U.S. interests, there is strong opposition to any such reopening among key segments of the Saudi and Kuwaiti populations. This opposition must be taken into account so that pursuit of the investment program does not fuel anti-Americanism in these countries or destabilize their ruling regimes.

6. Review Oil Sanctions Policy to Identify Ways to Reduce the Negative Impact on Energy Supplies While Accomplishing the Objectives for Which the Sanctions Were Imposed

More oil could likely be brought into the marketplace in the coming years if oil-field development could be enhanced by participation of U.S. companies in countries where such investments are currently banned, particularly in Libya where frozen U.S. assets remain in limbo. Resources are large and, with major contributions of foreign investment capital, large additions to production rates could be accrued in the coming two to three years.

Efforts should be made through cooperation and collaboration with Congress to phase out or drop sanctions that are no longer relevant to U.S. strategic objectives. Sanctions regimens that are ineffective should be reevaluated and restructured to increase their chances of producing the desired outcomes. An easing of sanctions in any particular country might conflict with other U.S. policy goals and must be reviewed in this context. However, the costs of prolonging these sanctions, both in terms of energy policy and foreign policy, must also be taken into account. The government needs to weigh arguments that sanctions are needed to restrain revenues of regimes whose policies are hostile to U.S. interests against the reality that imposition of oil sanctions on too many regimes at once can be ineffective and can have cumulative adverse effects. When they are effective they can also reduce market competition and contribute to overall higher oil price levels, higher U.S. vulnerability to disruption, and higher revenues for the very same adversaries. The latter can especially be the case when world markets are tight and other suppliers will not or are unable to increase supply to make up for the loss from the sanctioned country.

7. Develop a Credible International Stance on Global Warming and Other Environmental Issues

The United States lacks a clear and consistent policy reconciling energy and environmental objectives, and this is a large deficit in both U.S. domestic and foreign policy. Attempts to integrate energy and environmental policy continue to be hampered by the existence of market externalities, in which the true social costs of consumption of different fuel sources are not reflected in their purchase price. It is important in fashioning policy to clearly define externalities and environmental objectives from the outset. Environmental economic measures must tackle pollution at the point where it occurs, and such measures should also be deemed to have significant effect. They should be based on sound science and not constitute a tax on general economic activity. Thus, some specialists advocate that "green" taxes should be revenue neutral, except when spent on related activities, such as cleanups. Tradable permits can be considered in cases where tax solutions offer a strong policy alternative. Cleaner fuels should face a lower fiscal burden than those that have higher negative environmental consequences and thereby impose real costs and social burdens.

- a. *Conduct a thorough review of the Kyoto Accords and recommend ways for the United States to revive international discussions on climate change and also execute bilateral agreements with regard to promoting environmental safeguards.*

    A greater U.S. commitment on the global warming issue can help demonstrate seriousness regarding environmental issues, which have become central concerns of the international community. A strong U.S. international commitment can build on the strong U.S. domestic record on environmental matters, especially at a time when some more limited immediate environmental regulations might have to be waived temporarily to defend or de-bottleneck energy supply.

- b. *Investigate new ways to promote efficiency and clean energy technologies, including clean coal, expanded natural gas use, and automobile mileage and emission standards, for use in large consuming countries in Latin America and Asia, especially China and India.*

    Programs can include joint research on safer, proliferation-proof nuclear technologies, clean coal, renewable technologies, and alternative fuel automotive design. The IEA program on energy efficiency education and technology transfer should be expanded, and education programs on energy conservation practices should be developed not only inside U.S. public schools but also for governments and schools in other countries such as Russia, the former Soviet Union, China, India, etc.

- c. *Develop a strategy to coordinate with the European Union and the Association of Southeast Asian Nations*

(ASEAN) on refined petroleum product specifications through multilateral dialogue and bilateral agreements.

Just as better coordination is required between environmental regulators and energy policy officials nationally, so too should better coordination between these authorities be promoted on an international level. The issue of market Balkanization referred to earlier in these recommendations exists on an international level as well as on a national level. Lack of coordination on both product specifications and the timing of their introduction into the market have an important impact on trade and on pockets of supply shortages internationally. Better coordination would mean that shortfalls in one country could be rebalanced more easily by exports from another. This will help smooth localized price volatility and create more orderly international products trade.

8. Support Efforts to Develop and Disseminate Timely and Accurate Information about the Fundamentals of Energy Market Supply and Demand

Market efficiency and the smooth transition to deregulated energy supply and price are highly dependent upon adequate market signals and information. Yet ironically, in the information age, in which technology and communications advances have facilitated the development and dissemination of data, there has been a perceived decline in market transparency.

One of the major roles of public authorities in assuring the smooth functioning of markets now centers on the provision of data and information to facilitate market transparency. So far, this important role for governments has been under-recognized. There are clear obstacles to market transparency, and these will be hard to eliminate. These include the following:

- Restructuring of industry, with new "nontraditional" enterprises emerging that have not reported fundamentals to government (e.g., Independent Power Producer—IPPs—in the United States).

- Restructuring of industry, with loss of old reporting functions in some companies.
- Lack of government commitment to collecting data.
- Increased role of nonindustrialized societies in the global energy sector, with lack of data collection and development infrastructure.
- Decline of data collection integrity with the collapse of the Soviet Union, at a time when Russia and the successor states are more integrated into global energy markets.
- Refusal of some governments, most importantly oil producing countries including Saudi Arabia and Venezuela, to provide fundamental transparent information on supplies to markets, capacity to produce, reserves, and levels of inventories.

As a result, neither companies nor governments are receiving adequate and timely information at a time when markets are more volatile and more subject to large price movements. They are often making inappropriate decisions affecting the public good largely because their information base is wrong, threatening stable, affordable energy prices and reliable supply. It is widely agreed that the most reliable data are those compiled by the IEA. Yet there is widespread distrust of the integrity of IEA data, not only in OPEC and in the developing world but within OECD countries as well. Recognizing this, recently the Saudi government proposed establishing a permanent global institution in Riyadh to bridge differences between exporting countries and others. Yet Riyadh has acted in the past to thwart a transparent energy system. The commitment of Saudi Arabia to promote data transparency should be explored and tested by the administration.

- Recognizing that transparency is an important element in maintaining orderly markets generally and in times of energy or unexpected disruption in particular, the administration should provide a higher budget for the Department of Energy's Energy Information Agency.

    The agency needs to strengthen its ability to collect domestic data on all aspects of market fundamentals in order to restore the integrity of information on the U.S. market, a critical step in enhancing market transparency. It should work together with the IEA to improve the world-wide energy database, including data on fundamentals for all primary energy sources, including country specific data. The DOE should also investigate how to support and promote the sharing of accurate data among major oil-producing and oil-consuming countries through private or multilateral Internet publishing, publications, or regional organizations.

9. Lay the Foundation for New Global Energy Institutions
If the domestic and international goals of U.S. energy policy are to be maximized, it is time for the United States to consider revitalizing and revamping the international mechanisms governing international investment and trade in energy.

The United States should try to lay the institutional framework of new international energy institutions. The institutions should be designed to achieve such goals as:
- *Greater Transparency.* If the general goal of U.S. energy policy is the perfection of markets so that investments can be made efficiently on a global basis in energy resources, that goal must start with transparency. (See recommendation 9 above.)
- *Rules of Trade and Investment.* At an international level, the energy sector has retained far more of the elements of the pre-free trade and investment environment of the 1920s and 1930s than any other sector, save, perhaps, agriculture. It is, at the core, a highly politicized sector. Efforts to defuse those politics have been relatively unsuccessful. There is little doubt that the objectives of securing diversified energy resources on a diversified geographic basis would be fostered by the adoption of international rules governing trade and investment in energy resources. Nor is there much doubt that as societies have abandoned the critical elements of resource nationalism, the basics are increasingly in place for the establishment of such rules.
- *Keeping Energy and Other Issues on Separate Tracks.* One of the major benefits of establishing institutions through which governments agree to a set of rules governing their mutual

arrangements for trade and investment is that through these rules governments would virtually explicitly be renouncing the use of energy as instruments of foreign policy for non-energy purposes. The energy world would parallel the world of the General Agreement on Tariffs and Trade (GATT) and the World Trade Organization. Governments would effectively agree to most-favored-nation principles of trade and investment and would thereby forswear the use of energy as an instrument of foreign policy against others party to the agreements. For example, neither oil producers/exporters nor oil importers would be able to embargo or boycott—with impunity—trade or capital flows with other agreed parties. Such a rule would civilize the energy sector much as other sectors of international trade and investment have been civilized, with disputes settled about the sector per se, not about exogenous issues.

The issue for the United States is not so much whether such new international institutions are desirable. Rather, it is how to achieve them. But it is clear that unless the United States assumes a leadership role in the formation of new rules of the game, it will not simply forfeit such a role, which others will assume. It will rather become reactive to initiatives put forth by other governments that, if agreed by others, could leave U.S. firms, consumers, and the government in a weaker position than is warranted. This could be already happening, for example, with respect to the establishment of a new information base for energy, given the commitment of the Saudi government to house such a base within its borders. It could also be happening with respect to the European Energy Charter, if Moscow agrees to ratify the Energy Charter treaty. In addition, such an effort would assist in preventing the emergence of international groupings of countries that could be antithetical to U.S. interests—for example an effort by Venezuela, Iraq, and Russia to align their interests against the United States on a host of international energy and nonenergy issues.

    a. *Embrace the spirit of "producer-consumer" dialogue, but not the framework with which it has been associated.* The idea of a broadly based and ongoing dialogue of oil producers and consumers, graced by the presence of big oil companies, has increasingly moved back into the international limelight. It has been reinforced by the spirit of cooperation between key OPEC and non-OPEC countries working together on production constraints and working with key oil-importing countries on an implicit understanding over a "just price" for oil. OPEC governments have been pushing this theme for several reasons: volatility in oil prices; the collapse of oil prices and revenues in 1998; and high consumer taxes on petroleum products in Europe and Japan. Producers, including non-OPEC members Mexico and Oman, argued that a handful of relatively poor developing countries were forced to assume unfairly an extraordinary burden of adjustment to lower oil prices. They argued that those benefiting from the lower prices had an obligation to both understand their plight and assist them in doing something about it. It was for this reason that most OPEC countries were sympathetic to the U.S. government's use of SPR time-swaps in 2000 to help damp the price peaks of the autumn of 2000. OPEC's position has been straightforward: OPEC cannot, by itself, bring stability to oil markets. Collaboration is needed both with other producing countries and with importing country governments, especially on thorny issues related to information on fundamentals, including the level of and management of inventories. The issues of this dialogue are global, but the framework won't work: market-based countries such as the United States cannot guarantee price floors; producer countries with limited output capacity cannot guarantee price ceilings. There can be no such bargain. Additionally, most OPEC governments do not want to see markets left to operate without government intervention. Some OPEC countries want not just a floor price, but a gradually rising one, however anti-competitive and administratively difficult this may be to enforce.

b. *With U.S. leadership, foster broad international cooperation on a host of issues, including 1) sharing information on oil market trends and the basics on evolving environmen-*

tal standards on petroleum products and emissions; 2) promoting mechanisms for attracting investment capital; and 3) coordinating information on investments in refinery upgrading and in new demand, which would define the requirements for new grassroots plants. The question is, How should appropriate global arrangements be institutionalized for a globalized world energy sector?

c. *Build global energy institutions in three ways:*

1. Consider using the European Energy Charter as the basis of the sort of energy institutions that the United States should want to adopt on a global basis. The original idea of a single European energy market extending from the Atlantic to Siberia, put forward in 1990, was that once unleashed by Western investments, ex-Soviet oil and gas resources could make Europe virtually self-sufficient, ending dependence on the Middle East.

    The main weakness of the original European scheme has always been that it takes a long time to get from here to there. Ex-Soviet output has languished; the rule of law has yet to be put in place in Russia; and no appropriate administrative procedure has been developed in any of the successors to the Soviet Union. Moscow has yet to ratify the treaty. The United States and Canada and Norway and Japan all had fears of being left in the cold, and wavered between joining and killing off the plan before it took root. But the Energy Charter put in place exactly the genre of rules the United States should want to seek, covering investment, trade, third-party transit, and fundamental environmental standards in member countries. The United States was unable, however, to sign the final texts because the EU members included certain stipulations—West-West issues as they were known—that were impossible to ratify because they touched on constitutionally fundamental federal/state divisions of labor that were impossible to overcome.

    It is time to re-examine the European Energy Charter as the basis of the sort of energy institution that the United States should want to adopt on a global basis. The

United States should take the lead to help forge a document that is in line with its interests and free from the problems of the past restrictions.

2. Build on overlapping interests and relations between the world's largest oil exporter (Saudi Arabia) and the largest energy consuming country (the United States). Immediately after the end of the Gulf War, the two countries had a once-in-a-generation opportunity to put in place the elements of a new institution governing oil trade. They failed to take advantage of that window of opportunity. Nonetheless, the elements of an agreement between the two superpowers of energy are worth considering; they could enhance not only Saudi and U.S. energy security, but that of much of the rest of the world as well. It could also help to assure the smooth operation of market forces and the needed growth in international oil trade and the energy trade in general. What is more, this process could work without either country undermining its respective partners in OPEC or the IEA.

    Negotiation of a bilateral agreement might start by fleshing out the long-standing Saudi call for a system of "reciprocal energy security." In return for even modest demonstrations of goodwill toward their country, Saudi ministers have suggested that the United States and other consumer nations could gain guaranteed access to "a fairly priced ocean of oil." A dialogue between the two countries could focus initially on short-term mechanisms designed to mitigate the economic damage caused by extreme oil price volatility. One element could be bilateral planning for strategic oil storage and use.

3. Explore a mechanism promoting a North American or Western Hemispheric energy agreement. NAFTA in many ways lays the groundwork for an internationally expanded energy sector. Trade in energy—in oil, natural gas, and electricity—is considered a central feature for the NAFTA agenda. The NAFTA-style framework could serve as a starting point for extension of its ener-

gy stipulations southward into Central and Latin America, at least where energy issues are concerned. The main impediment to pursuing an expanded NAFTA in energy on a hemispheric and global basis has resided both in the Mexican political refusal to consider amending its constitution to permit foreign investment in its energy sector and in resistance from Canada.

As with Saudi Arabia, the United States has a major decision to confront with respect to Mexico. Should the United States, in the process of pursuing more secure access to more energy resources, more assertively pressure its energy trading partners to open their sectors to foreign investment? Or should it remain passive about such a decision, respecting the objectives of those countries that chose to maintain a monopoly over their domestic energy resources? Whichever route chosen by the U.S. government, long-range commercial links will remain critical to reestablishing market stability in the petroleum sector. They are equally central to making sure that the next time a supply glut develops, the burden of adjusting to it is more equitably spread around the world.

4. Form the core of future multilateral agreements through bilateral or regional arrangements based on improving markets, ensuring energy security, and guaranteeing investments and trade on a mutual, reciprocal, and nondiscriminatory basis. The benefits first captured by the United States and Saudi Arabia in a bilateral agreement, or by the United States, Canada, and Mexico in a NAFTA agreement, or by signatories to an Energy Charter, could be progressively enlarged with similar agreements signed with other countries.

Building new international institutional arrangements in the new century will not be easy. But it is by no means impossible. It need not require the dismantling of OPEC or the IEA. Equally important, it need not require a politically difficult dialogue between the two organizations, a broader U.N. forum, or another setting for grand but fruitless discussions. Yet over time it could supersede all of these. It could provide the foundation for a kind of General Agreement of Petroleum and Petroleum Products, and Natural Gas, and Electricity. That is how the General Agreement on Tariffs and Trade emerged from bilateral trade agreements based on the extension of most-favored-nation treatment to a broad array of countries.

ACTION PLAN

The Task Force recommends a two-part action plan. The first stage consists of immediate actions to establish appropriate mechanisms to manage potential supply disruptions and to buffer the economy against harm from price volatility. The second part, consisting of longer-term actions, tackles the causes of recent shortfalls and emergencies. These initiatives establish a framework for developing new supplies and ample capacities along various linked global energy supply chains, while preserving and enhancing the human habitat.

IMMEDIATE ACTIONS

There are few options available to government to expand supply in the short run or to reduce short-term demand. Consequently, immediate actions should consider all possible means of de-bottlenecking supplies and reducing obstacles to delivery of supplies, both domestically and internationally. In addition, the short-term actions must establish permanent machinery for integrating energy policy with economic, environmental, national security, and foreign policies. To the degree that new supplies alleviate energy shortfalls in periods of peak demand, they will provide protection to consumers against price spikes.

Virtually all actions available to remove obstacles along the supply chain in the very short term involve tradeoffs with other policy objectives, including environmental, national security, and foreign policy concerns. Therefore, tradeoffs must be carefully weighed. Any supply-side relief also eliminates the only current mechanism for controlling demand: higher prices. Proper policy must consider measures that will prevent the public from keeping U.S. energy security perpetually beyond reach. For the immediate and short term, two sorts of policies need to be considered:

- Those that quickly alleviate supply bottlenecks and damp demand.
- Those that need to be adopted in a timely manner in order to have a desirable impact in the longer term, given the long lead times required in order to mobilize capital or new technologies.

Key elements of this plan are designed to:

- safeguard supply in times of accident or disruption to ensure orderly markets.
- ease and eventually eliminate constraints in the energy infrastructure.
- promote diversity of clean, fairly priced, abundant supply sources.
- enhance energy efficiency and curb unbridled growth of energy consumption.
- ensure fair competition and market solutions.
- promote restructuring of formal institutions and informal arrangements for managing international energy relations.

Steps
1. Deter and manage international supply shortfalls.
   a. Develop a diplomatic program ensuring GCC allies remain prepared and willing to maintain stable prices for global economic growth and also to fill any unexpected supply shortfalls in times of turmoil in the oil markets, whether created by accident or by adverse political actions on the part of any producing nation.
   b. Prepare for contingencies and gain agreement on coordination in the IEA in efforts to deal with any removal of oil by adversary nations from international markets.
   c. Minimize public conflicts with OPEC and other independent oil-exporting countries but emphasize importance of market factors in setting prices.
   d. While moving to defuse tensions in the Arab-Israeli conflict through conflict resolution and negotiations, maintain energy and political issues in U.S.-Middle East relations on separate tracks.

e. Review policies toward Iraq to lower anti-Americanism in the Middle East and elsewhere; set the groundwork to eventually ease Iraqi oil-field investment restrictions.

2. Remove bottlenecks and other obstacles to energy supply, both domestically and internationally.
   a. Streamline procedures for waiving product specifications.
   b. Establish procedures to grant Jones Act waivers without adversely affecting U.S. ship owners or U.S. labor.
   c. Enact legislation for federal primacy over state regulations especially with respect to product specifications and pipeline right of way.
   d. Enact legislation to facilitate regional solutions to energy challenges.
   e. Investigate whether any changes in U.S. policy would rapidly facilitate higher Caspian Basin oil exports.

3. Take a fresh approach to building and maintaining national strategic and commercial crude oil and petroleum product inventories.
   a. Review the size and financing of the SPR.
   b. Establish professional criteria for managing the SPR.
   c. Establish clear policy for use of the SPR.
   d. Review tax, accounting, and other factors affecting industry's incentives to hold petroleum product and natural gas inventories with the intent of enhancing inventories before seasonal demand, and neutralizing any adverse impact of current rules.
   e. Encourage states to review minimum inventory for fuel switching where feasible and also fiscal incentives to industry to build inventories in advance of seasonal demand increases.

4. Develop mechanisms for a new national approach to energy policy.
   a. Create an appropriate interagency process to articulate and promote energy security policy and integrate energy policy with overall economic, environmental, and foreign policy.
   b. Review and streamline the allocation of authorities within the federal government, especially in areas of land management and energy.

c. Convene a national energy security summit to help develop a national consensus on energy policy objectives and means.

d. Develop a strategic communications plan on energy security policy in order to educate the public on the difficulties of achieving short-term, unilateral solutions to the nation's energy dilemmas.

LONG-TERM POLICY INITIATIVES

1. Review international approaches to build, maintain, and use strategic and commercial crude oil and petroleum product inventories.

   a. Enhance and modernize IEA strategic stockpile policies in light of the changed international market, taking into account situations that technically fall short of a supply disruption as well as different regulatory authorities among IEA members.

   b. Encourage key non-IEA countries (e.g., China, India, Brazil) to develop strategic stocks.

   c. Review IEA membership, taking into account the desirability of creating a new class of associated members who could be encouraged to hold minimum stocks and also benefit from direct participation in other IEA activities.

2. Accelerate demand-management efforts at home and internationally.

   a. Take a proactive government position on demand management.

   b. Use federal procurement authority to promote use of alternative fuels, and develop programs to introduce new efficiency technologies into federal buildings and nascent transportation technologies into government vehicle fleets.

   c. Use federal procurement authority to achieve other demand management goals.

   d. Review and establish new and stricter CAFE mileage standards, especially for light trucks.

e. Actively promote the development of energy-efficient technologies, including fuel-efficient engine and vehicle technologies.

3. Maximize efforts to develop every clean source of domestic fuel supply.

   a. Oil and natural gas

      1. Accelerate completion of the U.S. oil and natural gas reserve inventory, as mandated by Congress, paying special attention to restrictions on resource development. Such an inventory needs to be completed soon and well before any plan is adopted to develop particular domestic resources.

      2. Undertake an accelerated and complete review of tax and fiscal policy as they impact U.S. oil and gas development, taking into account the competitive position of the U.S. fiscal regime internationally, in order to attract more capital to the sector.

   b. Power (Electricity)

      1. Create an appropriate, comprehensive statutory framework for electricity restructuring and for reestablishing a capacity cushion for the nation's power supplies. A new framework needs to overcome the adverse impacts of today's highly fragmented regime, which has reduced the reliability of power grid and impeded investment in new generation and transmission capacity.

      2. Work expeditiously to improve the statutory framework for approvals of the siting of power generation plants, and transmission and distribution infrastructure.

      3. Evaluate the need for incentives to stimulate the introduction of new technologies into the power marketplace, including distributed generation and co-generation.

      4. Work with state regulators and regional authorities to let companies offer long-term contracts for electric power and to encourage them to hedge price risks.

      5. Encourage the development of regional power capacity cushions.

      6. Recognize that many of the polices required to meet increased demand are power-source specific.

7. Assure that regulations protect open access to electricity generated by new nontraditional fuel sources.
c. Natural Gas
   1. Apply strong leadership to develop a coherent, comprehensive strategy promoting efficient development and use of the nation's natural gas resources.
   2. Endorse the construction of natural gas pipelines from the Arctic to the lower forty-eight states and work bilaterally with Canada and Alaska to address important issues that need to be resolved.
   3. Assure regulatory authorities work together to bring about natural gas market efficiencies, including the provision of open access to markets by producers and to supply by end users, and that allow delivery costs to be determined transparently by market forces so that commodity values are transparent to both producers and consumers.
   4. Invest in—or stimulate and encourage private sector investment in—research and development of technologies that focus on safe and cost-effective ultra-deep water production, smaller drilling footprints, and increased production from nonconventional sources, including methane hydrates.
   5. Encourage natural gas exploration and production through a series of technology-targeted tax incentives that also encourage use of advanced, environmentally sensitive technologies, and that provide counter-cyclical support for exploration and production.
   6. Initiate a mitigation forum process to evaluate infrastructure needs and reduce delays in new pipeline and storage facility siting.
   7. Consider providing incentives to state and local governments that agree to expedite natural gas infrastructure siting.
   8. Invest in—or stimulate and encourage private-sector investment in—technologies ensuring pipeline infrastructure integrity, reliability, flexibility, and safety.

9. Foster development of advanced storage technologies to increase regional storage capacity and serve peak power and distributed-generation markets.

10. Evaluate the potential of imported liquefied natural gas as a major additional source of base load as well as incremental supply, and in the process accelerate environmental reviews required for siting as well as accommodate the commercial logistics and other user needs associated with facilities built or operated by LNG suppliers.

d. Coal: Given the nation's abundance in coal resources it is critical to foster the development of clean coal technologies to promote coal use in power generation, while mitigating the impacts of coal combustion to meet local, regional, and global environmental challenges.

e. Nuclear

1. Support the Nuclear Regulatory Commission to extend plant life where possible.

2. Constructively work with stakeholders to resolve nuclear power plant spent fuel (and high-levels defense waste) disposition within the next few years, since this is critical to preserving viable nuclear options for the nation.

3. Work to improve the investment climate for new nuclear power plant construction through NRC streamlining of licensing procedures and by resolving uncertainties surrounding electricity deregulation and restructuring.

4. Work with Congress to sustain the front-end domestic nuclear fuel cycle through the next half-decade.

5. Work with Japan and allies in Western Europe to shape a future nuclear fuel cycle that would garner shared support.

6. Work with the education system to reinvigorate training in nuclear science and technology.

4. Augment diplomatic initiatives to spur non-OPEC production increases.

a. Expand Oil and Gas Forum programs.

b. Investigate ways to facilitate increased investment in Mexico's oil and gas sectors.

   c. Encourage reforms in Russia's energy sector.

   d. Improve access to information and transparency on comparative oil and gas fiscal/commercial regimes.

5. Initiate diplomatic efforts to encourage the reopening of countries that have nationalized and monopolized their upstream sectors.

6. Review sanctions policies, to identify ways to reduce the negative impact on energy supplies while accomplishing the objectives for which the sanctions were imposed.

7. Develop a credible international stance on global warming and other environmental issues.

   a. Conduct a thorough review of the Kyoto Accords and recommend ways for the United States to revive international discussions on climate change and also execute bilateral agreements to promote environmental safeguards.

   b. Investigate new ways to promote efficiency and clean energy technologies, including clean coal, expanded natural gas use, and automobile mileage and emission standards, for use in large consuming countries in Latin America and Asia, especially China and India.

   c. Develop a strategy to coordinate with the European Union and the Association of Southeast Asian Nations (ASEAN) on refined petroleum product specifications through multilateral dialogue and bilateral agreements.

8. Support efforts to develop and disseminate accurate and timely information about the fundamentals of energy market supply and demand. The administration should recognize that transparency is an important element in maintaining orderly markets generally and in times of emergency or unexpected disruption in particular, and thus should provide a higher budget for the Department of Energy's Energy Information Agency.

9. Lay the foundation for new global energy institutions.

   a. Embrace the spirit of the "producer-consumer" dialogue but not the framework with which it has been associated.

   b. With U.S. leadership, foster broad international cooperation on a host of issues including (1) sharing information on oil market trends and the basics of evolving environmental standards on petroleum products and emissions; (2) promoting mechanisms for attracting investment capital; and (3) coordinating information on investments in refinery upgrading and in new demand, which would define the requirements for new grassroots plants.

c. Build global energy institutions in three ways:

   1. Consider using the European Energy Charter as the basis of an energy institution that the United States should want to adopt on a global basis.

   2. Build on overlapping interests and relations between the world's largest oil exporter (Saudi Arabia) and the largest energy-consuming country (the United States).

   3. Explore a mechanism promoting a North American or Western Hemispheric energy agreement.

d. Form the core of a future multilateral agreement through bilateral or regional arrangements based on improving markets, ensuring energy security, and guaranteeing investments and trade on a mutual, reciprocal, and nondiscriminatory basis.

ADDITIONAL VIEWS

On Environmental Considerations, Coordinated Energy and Environmental Policy, Federal and State Jurisdictions, and Enhanced Demand-Side Measures

Energy policy is a derivative policy—deriving from our security, economic, and environmental goals. These are often in conflict. It is therefore difficult to chart an energy policy path that is coherent and on which consensus can be achieved. Although supportive of many conclusions in the report, we are generally more sanguine than the report regarding the ability of the market, especially under current prices, to bring forth necessary increases in supply for oil and gas. We would place primary emphasis on attending to those infrastructure and volatility issues that are principally governmental in origin and solution. We would also like to emphasize the need for government action in certain areas. These include:

- The need to focus international discussions on atmospheric *concentrations* of greenhouse gases.
- The development of a coordinated energy and environmental policy that includes specific attention to carbon dioxide and incentives for voluntary early action activities. Unless carbon dioxide is addressed, and addressed in a way that is credible with major domestic constituencies and with others internationally, the environmental regime will remain unstable, increasing investment uncertainty and hence raising energy costs—all this quite apart from one's judgments about environmental impacts.
- A legislative rebalancing of the boundaries between federal and state jurisdictions to increase federal and regional influence over environmentally based standards and within the electric power sector. The purpose of such a move would be to establish and enforce a consistent and efficient transmission and reliability regime applicable to all industry participants.

- Efforts to enhance efficiency. Efficiency has a critical role in balancing supply and demand. An analysis by the President's Committee of Advisors on Science and Technology has shown that from 1970 to 2000, improvements in the overall efficiency in the U.S. energy system (measured as real GNP divided by primary energy supplied) saved two and one-half times more energy than the growth of all sources of supply combined.
- Increased federal support of research and development related to energy and environmental technologies on both the demand and supply sides in order to sustain a stable economic environment for energy, to accommodate economic growth, and to meet environmental objectives. Technology has been critical to energy development in the past and will continue to be so in the future.
- Enhanced demand-side measures, including incentives for the accelerated introduction of technology. More effective strategies for the deployment of existing technologies can in particular make a significant difference. In electric power markets, regulation must make demand sensitive to the cost of power if those markets are to work properly. In other markets, the report calls for regulatory intervention to achieve demand restraint, presumably on the unstated assumption that Americans will not tolerate the use of taxes even though, we note, taxes would often be a more efficient instrument of control.

Finally, we caution against using the "crisis" label, which in the past has been the source of much energy policy mischief. Apart from the very serious problems in the California and western electricity markets, which largely derive from policy, current energy markets are not in "crisis," and precipitous action should not undermine thoughtful resolution of our conflicting energy, economic, environmental, and security concerns.

Graham Allison
Joseph C. Bell
Charles B. Curtis

On Nuclear Energy

Nuclear power is an indigenous source of energy—invented and developed in America. It is unique in having the capacity to provide enough energy to last our nation—and the world—for at least a millennium. And it can do so without emitting greenhouse gases. Nuclear energy should not be considered as an option, but as a necessity to supply electricity for the nation now and in the future. The Energy Information Administration has predicted that between now and 2020, the United States will need 300,000 megawatts of additional generating capacity, or the equivalent of three hundred large new plants of any type. A minimum of one hundred fifty of these plants should be nuclear.

Michel T. Halbouty

On Efficiency

Between 1973 and 1986, the U.S. economy's energy intensity (energy consumption per dollar of GDP) declined by 35 percent; since then, the rate of decline slowed dramatically, amounting to only about 15 percent over the period. That slowdown raises total national energy costs by about $100 billion per year. Technologies are in hand to once again accelerate energy efficiency and associated environmental gains significantly. To realize this in a timely way requires that integrated fiscal, regulatory, and technology policies be implemented by the administration and Congress. In addition, the government should use its own procurement activities far more aggressively to develop a reasonable domestic market for new clean and efficient technologies and alternative fuels. It should also work with the private sector and international financial institutions to advance associated deployment in developing countries. Such actions, in creating stable markets adequate to permit private development of alternative technologies and infrastructure, can be an important element of energy security policy and reduce upside price volatility. They fall into the category of "public good" actions addressing market shortcomings. Opportunities are clearly available in both the transportation and electricity sectors. Such demand-side initiatives can have a substantially greater impact than supply-side initiatives on the overall supply/demand balance over the next several years. However, the importance of stability to the success of such initiatives requires a pragmatic joint administration-congressional commitment.

On Diplomacy

In regard to dealing with oil-producing nations during periods of oil price volatility, the report properly emphasizes the importance of quiet diplomatic discussion and a bedrock principle of reliance on market forces. However, the administration, confronted with nonmarket behavior, also needs to retain the flexibility to use all diplomatic tools of engagement, including appropriate use of public statements. For example, such diplomatic engagement during the last year saw significant production increases while holding in place key international support for use of the SPR to address inventory shortfalls and associated price volatility.

On Critical Infrastructure Protection

Protecting our energy infrastructure from being disabled is an energy security concern of increasing importance. Heightened vulnerability to physical and/or cyber disruption stems from increased infrastructure interdependence, increased risk of cascading failures, and increased reliance on information technologies and telecommunications in the energy infrastructure. An appropriate response demands new forms of cooperation between the private sector, local governments, and the federal government, including robust and timely exchange of sensitive information on both sides. The critical infrastructure protection initiative of the last few years needs substantial upgrading in order to better coordinate with infrastructure interdependencies, provide realistic evolving vulnerability assessments, develop technologies to protect control systems, develop and deploy integrated multisensor detection systems to warn of system disruption, and lower institutional barriers to the associated public-private coordination activities. A significant increase in federal research and development funding for energy infrastructure protection is needed.

Melanie A. Kenderdine
Ernest J. Moniz

On Tax Incentives, Demand Efficiency, the SPR, and Reserve Capacity

Based on the serious energy supply problems facing the United States and in view of past national energy policy initiatives (starting in the Nixon administration), the greatest emphasis has always been focused on increasing supply of traditional fuels. Also overlooked is the fact that the tax code has been extraordinarily favorable to the exploration, production, and development of oil, natural gas, and coal, and that the federal government has subsidized the development of nuclear power far more than it has solar, wind, and other clean alternatives.

It is also obvious that there is little need to provide any tax or other incentive to the oil and gas industry. The major companies are reporting record profits and prices are at very high levels. Consumers—especially low- and moderate-income consumers—are suffering from the high cost of natural gas and other heating fuels. Furthermore, many low-income households are facing utility cutoffs because of the sharp increase in heating costs. These problems require immediate solution—from sharply increasing low-income heating assistance and weatherization programs to prohibiting shut-offs.

While the report does recommend demand-side energy efficiency initiatives, I believe that such initiatives can go much further. Tax incentives for building energy-efficient homes and buildings, installing energy-efficient equipment, and purchasing energy-efficient appliances would create a vigorous market for energy efficient products. On-the-shelf energy-efficient technologies are available. Expanding U.S. production of energy-efficient technologies will also enhance our domestic economy and provide new opportunities for exports.

While I support the report's recommendations regarding the building of the SPR, it is also important to define clearly when it should be used. Essentially, rapid increases in price are a sign of market failure. An emergency situation calling for use of the SPR could be defined as a percentage increase in price within a specified period of time—say, 25 percent over ten or fifteen days.

It is also critical to determine a requirement for companies that refine and import petroleum to hold a certain level of stock. As the report correctly points out, deregulation and reliance on the market does not ensure supply security. Previously, companies deemed it to be in their economic self-interest to hold inventory. Now, companies seek to hold as little inventory as possible in order to lower costs. This strategy of just-in-time inventory management has been very costly to consumers and the economy, and requires intervention by the federal government. While some may argue that we should rely on market forces to determine appropriate inventory levels, experience has confirmed that market forces are not working. Requiring all companies to hold a minimum level of inventory will provide at least some cushion of supply during periods of disruption.

A similar strategy ought to be applied to suppliers of natural gas, propane, and electricity. Deregulation of the electric utility market has left utility customers at the mercy of independent electricity generators who, unlike regulated utilities, have no incentive or requirement to build reserve capacity. The lack of reserve capacity, like the low levels of oil inventories, is a growing threat to consumers and the economy.

Ed Rothschild

On Demand Restraint

The "energy crisis" described in the report results in large part from the unconstrained growth of energy consumption. The United States is unique among the industrialized countries in that it does not use fiscal measures to limit growth in energy use. This policy must change to control growth of energy use and maintain environmental quality. The most efficient mechanism would be broad-based taxes on energy. In addition, the United States should consider imposing higher taxes on vehicles to encourage the expedited introduction of more efficient energy-using technology. These taxes should be introduced in a revenue-neutral fashion. In addition, regions such as California, which face energy disruptions due to infrastructure constraints, should consider replacing regressive sales taxes with taxes on energy designed to offset the infrastructure constraint.

On the Use of Strategic Stocks

The authors of the report are to be congratulated for their extensive discussion of the role of inventories. Industrialized countries must recognize that the increasingly competitive structure of the global economy prevents firms in the energy sector from holding reserve capacity (whether in the form of inventories or reserve generation capacity). Energy prices will be more volatile as a consequence. Governments must develop measures to compensate for this structural change if they wish to moderate the increase in the effect of price volatility. Such incentives can include more frequent use of governmentally owned inventories or the provisions of tax incentives to firms to build reserves. In planning such measures, governments should recognize that mandated stocks or imposition of reserve requirements by regulation generally are not effective. It must be understood that the cost of any measure designed to mitigate price volatility will be borne either by the taxpayer or the consumer. Efforts should be made to achieve the maximum reduction in volatility at a minimum cost.

Philip K. Verleger Jr.

DISSENTING VIEWS

On Caspian Energy Export Routes
Which export routes for Caspian energy are most appropriate depends primarily on which transit countries offer favorable conditions by facilitating construction of pipelines and charging reasonable transit fees. The actual pipeline construction cost is only one component—and not necessarily a large one—of any commercial decision about which route to use. The records of Russia and most especially Iran are of long delays and unreasonable demands. At this stage, the Baku-Ceyhan project is more advanced than any other oil pipeline project not yet under construction. In these circumstances, it is inappropriate to assume, as the report does, that promoting Baku-Ceyhan is at odds with a commercial approach toward Caspian energy.

Patrick Clawson
David L. Goldwyn

On Alternative Energy Sources, Minimum Petroleum Inventory Standards, an Organization of Petroleum Importing Countries, Nuclear Energy
U.S. energy policy should be guided by a stronger commitment to developing alternative energy sources and protecting vulnerable households and businesses from price shocks resulting from hikes in the costs of heating oil, gasoline, and diesel fuel.

Mandating minimum standards for petroleum inventories in the United States and creating an Organization of Petroleum Importing Countries (OPIC) to stand up to the Organization of Petroleum Exporting Countries are measures that should be taken to more aggressively protect our oil-dependent economy.

The establishment of federal minimum inventory standards for domestic wholesalers would buffer consumers from skyrocketing prices associated with inadequate inventories at times of high demand. In New England, for example, home heating oil prices went up $1 a gallon in the winter of 2000, when a severe cold snap combined with low inventories to send fuel costs through the roof. Similar supply shortages have resulted in soaring gasoline prices in the Midwest during the summer's peak demand months.

An OPIC to offset the clout of OPEC would use the threat of sanctions to keep the cartel from illegally manipulating production quotas to their advantage and our detriment. Moreover, OPIC would negotiate an end to radical price fluctuations that hurt producing and consuming nations alike by supporting a floor price for crude oil in exchange for OPEC backing of a ceiling price. A floor price of $20 a barrel would ensure adequate revenues to producing states, which depend on such dividends for their political, economic, and social stability. A ceiling price of $25 a barrel would guard against price shocks while encouraging the development of alternative energy sources in consuming nations.

U.S. policy guided by the goals of expanding nuclear capacity and exploiting domestic sources of oil and gas will not succeed in the long run. Energy independence is critical. This cannot be achieved by more drilling within U.S. borders. The only method is to increase our dependence on effective and affordable renewable energy sources in addition to creating a stable pricing environment for all our energy needs.

We must aggressively pursue promising alternative sources of energy to heat our homes, run our vehicles, and power our businesses. At the same time, we must take a tougher line toward the oil industry domestically to protect the most vulnerable, and use our clout internationally with oil producers to end the price shocks caused by their manipulation of oil markets.

Joseph P. Kennedy II

TASK FORCE MEMBERS

ODEH ABURDENE is managing partner of Capital Trust S.A. He was a manager in the international division of the American Security Bank in Washington, D.C., and served as a Vice President with the First National Bank of Chicago.

GRAHAM ALLISON is Director of the Belfer Center for Science and International Affairs at Harvard University's John F. Kennedy School of Government and Douglas Dillon Professor of Government. In the first term of the Clinton administration, he served as Assistant Secretary of Defense for Policy and Plans.

JOSEPH C. BELL is a Partner with Hogan & Hartson, L.L.P. He was previously U.S. Designated Representative for the International Energy Agency, Dispute Settlement Center; Assistant General Counsel of International Affairs for the Federal Energy Administration (1974–77); and the Cabinet Task Force on Oil Import Controls (1969).

PATRICK CLAWSON is Director for Research at the Washington Institute for Near East Policy and was previously a Senior Economist at the International Monetary Fund, the World Bank, and the National Defense University. He has written or edited twelve books about the Middle East.

FRANCES D. COOK heads the Ballard Group LLC, a business facilitation service in Washington. She is a three-time former ambassador, including twice to energy-exporting countries. She twice served as Deputy Assistant Secretary of State, where her specialty was political-military affairs.

JACK L. COPELAND is Chairman of Copeland Consulting International, an investment and geopolitical advisory firm.

CHARLES B. CURTIS is Senior Adviser to the United Nations Foundation and the President of NTI, a newly formed foundation organized to reduce the contemporary threat from weapons of mass destruction. He has previously served as the Deputy Secretary and the Undersecretary of the U.S. Department of Energy, the Chairman of the Federal Energy Regulatory Commission, and the Chief Energy Counsel of the U.S. House of Representatives' Energy and Commerce Committee.

TOBY T. GATI is Senior International Adviser at Akin, Gump, Strauss, Hauer & Feld, L.L.P. She served as Special Assistant to the President and Senior Director for Russia, Ukraine, and the Eurasian States at the National Security Council in 1993, and then as Assistant Secretary of State for Intelligence and Research until May 1997.

LUIS GIUSTI currently serves as Non-Executive Director of "Shell" Transport and Trading, and as Senior Adviser to the Center for Strategic and International Studies. Formerly, he was Chairman and CEO of Petróleos de Venezuela, S.A.

DAVID L. GOLDWYN is the principal of Goldwyn International Strategies, LLC, an international consulting firm. He served as Assistant Secretary of Energy for International Affairs and Counselor to the Secretary of Energy, Senior Adviser to the Permanent Representative to the United Nations, and Chief of Staff for the Undersecretary of State for Political Affairs under President Bill Clinton.

MICHEL T. HALBOUTY is an internationally renowned earth scientist and engineer whose career and accomplishments in the fields of geology and petroleum engineering have earned him the recognition as one of the world's outstanding geo-scientists.

AMY MYERS JAFFE is the senior energy adviser at the James A. Baker III Institute for Public Policy of Rice University and President of AMJ Energy Consulting. Formerly she was the senior economist and Middle East Analyst for *Petroleum Intel-*

ligence Weekly. Jaffe is the author of numerous articles on oil geopolitics, the Middle East, and the Caspian basin region.

MELANIE A. KENDERDINE is the Vice President of the Gas Technology Institute. Previously she was Director of Policy at the Department of Energy, Senior Policy Adviser to the Secretary of Energy for oil and gas, Deputy Assistant Secretary at Department of Energy, and Chief of Staff to Congressman Bill Richardson (D-N.M.).

JOSEPH P. KENNEDY II is Chairman and President of Citizens Energy Corporation, a nonprofit firm he founded in 1979 to provide low-cost heating oil to the poor and the elderly. He left Citizens in 1986 to serve six terms in the U.S. House of Representatives and returned to Citizens Energy full-time in 1999 and serves on the boards of companies in the health care, telecommunications, and energy industries.

MARIE-JOSEE KRAVIS is an Economist and Senior Fellow at the Hudson Institute. She specializes in trade and international finance-related issues and serves on the Secretary of Energy's Advisory Board. She also sits on the boards of Ford Motor Company, Vivendi Universal, U.S.A Networks, Hasbro Inc., Hollinger International, and the CIBC.

KENNETH LAY is Chairman and CEO of Enron Corporation. Lay also was CEO of Enron from 1985 until February 2001.

JOHN H. LICHTBLAU is Chairman and CEO of Petroleum Industry Research Foundation, Inc. (PIRINC). He has been a member of the National Petroleum Council (Advisory Council to the Secretary of Energy) since 1968 and is also a member of the International Associates of Energy Economics.

JOHN A. MANZONI is Regional President for British Petroleum in the eastern United States. Formerly he was Group Vice President for the Refining and Marketing business, and before that he headed up the BP side of the BP/Amoco merger directorate.

THOMAS F. MCLARTY III is Vice Chairman of Kissinger McLarty Associates, an international strategic advisory firm. He was President Bill Clinton's first Chief of Staff and also served as Counselor to the President and Special Envoy for the Americas. Prior to joining the Clinton administration, McLarty was Chairman and CEO of Arkla, Inc.

ERIC D.K. MELBY is a Senior Fellow with the Forum for International Policy and a principal in the Scowcroft Group. He handled economic and energy issues on the National Security Council staff from 1987–93 and was Special Assistant to the Executive Director of the International Energy Agency from 1981–85. He also worked in the Department of State and Agency for International Development.

SARAH MILLER is Editorial Vice President and Group Editor of the Energy Intelligence Group. She was European Director of McGraw-Hill News and London bureau chief and energy correspondent for McGraw-Hill World News.

STEVEN L. MILLER is Chairman of the board of directors, President, and CEO of Shell Oil Company. He is a member of the National Petroleum Council and the Business Roundtable.

ERNEST J. MONIZ is a Professor of Physics and former Head of the Department of Physics at the Massachusetts Institute of Technology. He served as Associate Director for Science in the Office of Science and Technology Policy in the Executive Office of the President (1995–97) and as Undersecretary for Energy, Science, and Environment in the Department of Energy (1997–2001). At the Department of Energy, he also served as the Secretary's Special Negotiator for Russian Programs.

EDWARD L. MORSE is Executive Advisor at Hess Energy Trading Co., LLC. He joined HETCO in April 1999 after more than a decade as Publisher of *Petroleum Intelligence Weekly*. From 1978 to 1981 Morse was at the Department of State, where he served as Deputy Assistant Secretary for international energy policy. A frequent commentator on oil market trends, both in writing and for broadcast media, Morse is the author or co-author of four books on politics, finance, energy, and international affairs.

SHIRLEY NEFF is an Economist for the Democrats on the Senate Energy and Natural Resources Committee. Prior to joining the committee staff, she was an economist for a state public utility commission and for an oil and gas company and an electricity utility.

DAVID O'REILLY is Chairman of the Board and CEO of Chevron-Texaco. Earlier, O'Reilly was one of the company's two Vice Chairmen, responsible for Chevron's worldwide exploration and production and corporate human relations.

KENNETH RANDOLPH is General Counsel and Secretary of Dynegy, Inc., responsible for all of Dynegy's legal and regulatory activities. Prior to joining Dynegy, he served as an energy attorney for the law firm of Akin, Gump, Strauss, Hauer & Feld in Washington, D.C.

PETER ROSENTHAL is Chief Correspondent on energy and commodities for *Bridge News*.

GARY N. ROSS is Chief Executive Officer of the PIRA Energy Group, a New York-based international energy consultancy retained by some three hundred companies in more than thirty countries.

ED ROTHSCHILD is Principal at the consulting firm of Podesta/Mattoon in Washington, D.C. Formerly the Energy Policy Director of Citizen Action and consumer advocate on energy matters from 1971–97, he is also the author of numerous reports and studies on natural gas and oil pricing issues, competition, and concentration in the petroleum industry.

JEFFERSON B. SEABRIGHT is Vice President of Policy Planning for Texaco, Inc. He was formerly the Executive Director of the White House Task Force on Climate Change, Director of the Office of Energy, Environment & Technology, and U.S. Agency for International Development.

Task Force Members

ADAM SIEMINSKI is the Director and Global Energy Strategist at Deutsche Banc Alex. Brown. From 1988–97, he was a Senior Equity Analyst for NatWest Securities, covering the major U.S.-based international oil companies.

MATHEW SIMMONS is President of Simmons & Company International, a specialized energy investment bank. He is a Member of the National Petroleum Council and Bush-Cheney Energy Transition Advisory Committee.

RONALD SOLIGO is a Professor of Economics at Rice University with a specialty in development and energy economics. He has authored a number of studies on energy-related topics for the James A. Baker III Institute for Public Policy at Rice University.

MICHAEL D. TUSIANI has been Chairman and CEO of Poten & Partners since 1983. Prior to joining Poten in 1973, he was employed by Zapata Naess Shipping Company. He has written two books: *The Petroleum Shipping Industry—A Non-Technical Overview* and *The Petroleum Shipping Industry—Operations and Practices*.

PHILIP K. VERLEGER JR. is President of PK Verleger LLC and a Principal with the Brattle Group. He served as an energy adviser in the Ford and Carter administrations and advised President Ronald Reagan on energy issues. He is the author of two books and numerous articles on the causes of energy price volatility.

ENZO VISCUSI is Group Senior Vice President and Representative for the Americas of Eni, the Italian-based integrated energy company, where he also serves as Chairman of Agip Petroleum Co., Inc.

CHUCK WATSON is the Chairman and CEO of Houston Dynegy Inc., a leading provider of energy and communications solutions. He established NGC Corp, Dynegy's predecessor, in 1985 and served as President until becoming Chairman and CEO in 1989.

WILLIAM H. WHITE is President of the Wedge Group Inc., a diversified investment firm with subsidiaries in the oil services, engineering, hotel, and real estate business. He is Chairman of the Houston World Affairs Council and served as deputy secretary and CEO of the U.S. Department of Energy from 1993 to 1995.

DANIEL YERGEN is Chairman of Cambridge Energy Research Associates. He is author of *The Prize*, for which he received the Pulitzer Prize, co-author of *The Commanding Heights*, and recipient of the U.S. Energy Award.

MINE YÜCEL is Senior Economist and Assistant Vice President, Federal Reserve Bank of Dallas. He is a member of the U.S. Association of Energy Economics and the author of numerous articles on energy and the economy.

TASK FORCE OBSERVERS

PAUL W. CHELLGREN is Chairman of the Board and Chief Executive Officer of Ashland, Inc. He is Director/Trustee at PNC Financial Services Group, Medtronic, Inc., the University of Kentucky, Center College, and American Petroleum Institute.

RICHARD N. COOPER is Maurits C. Boas Professor of International Economics at Harvard University. He was formerly Chairman of the National Intelligence Council, Federal Reserve Bank of Boston, and Undersecretary of State for Economic Affairs. He is the author of *The Economics of Interdependence* and other works.

CHARLES DUNCAN JR. serves on the boards of Newfield Exploration Company, Inc., and The Welch Foundation. He is Treasurer and Director of Methodist Health Care System, and Chairman of its subsidiary, Methodist Care, Inc. He was former Secretary of the Department of Energy from August 1979 until January 1981, and former President of the Coca-Cola Company.

WILLIAM E. HENDERSON III is manager, Joint Venture Coordination, Ashland, Inc.

JUDITH KIPPER is Director of the Council on Foreign Relations Middle East Forum and the Director of the Middle East Studies program at the Center for Strategic and International Studies.

ROBERT A. MANNING is the C.V. Starr Senior Fellow and Director of Asia Studies at the Council on Foreign Relations. He is the author of several books, including *The Asian Energy Factor: Myths and Dilemmas of Energy*. From 1989 until 1993, he was a Policy Adviser to the Assistant Secretary for East Asian and Pacific Affairs at the Department of State.

RICHARD MURPHY is Hasib J. Sabbagh Senior Fellow for the Middle East at the Council on Foreign Relations. He held successive appointments as Ambassador to Mauritania, Syria, the

Philippines, and Saudi Arabia. He served as Assistant Secretary of State for Near Eastern and South Asian Affairs.

STEPHEN OXMAN is a Senior Adviser, Morgan Stanley Dean Witter; former Assistant Secretary of State for European and Canadian Affairs; and former Partner with James D. Wolfensohn Incorporated.

MICHAEL L. TELSON has been Chief Financial Officer of the U.S. Department of Energy since October of 1997. He was Senior Analyst of the Committee on the Budget, U.S. House of Representatives, served as the Staff Economist of the House Ad Hoc Committee on Energy, and on the governing council of the International Association for Energy Economics (IAEE).

APPENDIXES

APPENDIX A

U.S. **Real GDP with Highlighted Oil Market Episodes, 1949-1999**

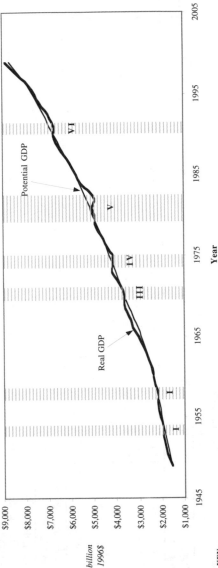

KEY:

I - Iranian national strikes by oil, coal, and steel workers. Effect: Oil price increases; GDP growth drops to -0.68% in 1954.

II - Suez Canal crisis. Effect: Oil price increases; GDP growth drops to -0.97% in 1958.

III - U.S. oil worker strikes (1969), OPEC production cutbacks (1970). Effect: Oil price increases; GDP growth slows to 0.18% i n 1970.

IV - OPEC oil embargo. Effect: Oil price increases; GDP growth drops to -0.59% in 1974 and -0.36% in 1975.

V - Iranian Revolution (1979), Iran-Iraq War (1980), and U.S. price decontrol (1981). Effect: Oil price rises; GDP growth drops to -0.23% in 1980 and -2.03% in 1982.

VI - Iraqi forces invade Kuwait. Effect: Oil price increases; GDP growth drops to -0.47% in 1991.

Sources: U.S. Federal Reserve (FRED Data Base), EIA Oil Market Analysis.

Appendix B: Past Oil Crises and Recent Issues Concerning Petroleum Security Guarantees

Reason	Crisis				
	First oil crisis (Oct. 1973)	*Second oil crisis* (Dec. 1978) (Oct. 1980)	*Iraq-Iran War*	*Gulf Crisis* (Aug. 1990)	*Present Market* 2000
	• Fourth Middle East war • Embargo by Arab oil producers	• Iranian revolution • Rapid oil production decreases in Iran • Iran-Iraq War	• Iraq attacks Iran	• Iraq invades Kuwait	• 1999 OPEC Agreement and Low Investment
Supply decrease period	• About 6 months	• About 4 months	• About 5 months	• About 7 months	• 12-months plus
Supply decrease magnitude	• 4.3~4.5 million B/D (2 months) • 2.2~2.6 million B/D (2 months)	• 5.3~5.6 million B/D (2 months) • 3.8 million B/D (2 months)	• 3.7~4.1 million B/D (2 months) • 2.5~3 million B/D (3 months)	• 5~5.3 million B/D (2 months) • 4~4.7 million B/D (3 months) • Total loss approx. 400~500 million barrels	• Over 1 billion barrels sustained Opec production cuts
Excess production capabilities	• About 3.75 million B/D	• About 4.55 million B/D	• About 6.7 million B/D	• About 6.2 million B/D	• 1-2 million B/D
No. of days of petroleum stocks in OECD	• Public: 0 • Private: 70 days	• Public: 7 days • Private: 65 days	• Public: 9 days • Private: 77 days	• Public: 25 days • Private: 61 days	• Public: 28 days • Private: 53 days

Petroleum market structure	• Majors posting price system • Majors rights in long-term crude contracts	• Sales pricing system by governments of oil-producing countries • Long-term contracts with oil-producing countries	• Sales pricing system by governments of oil-producing countries • Long-term contracts with oil-producing countries	• Market-linked pricing system • Development of oil futures market • Term contracts with oil-producing countries and expansion of spot transactions	• Market linked pricing system • Active oil futures market • Term contracts tied to spot transactions

Note: In the Gulf Crisis, reduced crude oil supplies continued even after the war had ended, until Kuwaiti production recovered.
Source: James A. Baker III Institute for Public Policy.

APPENDIX C

The following is excerpted from RADICAL POLITICS
by Adrian Binks
(March 26, 2001)
Petroleum Argus

The 'seventies are back. OPEC producers are warming to the rhetoric
that underlined Third World radicalism 30 years ago. Having suffered the destabilising consequences of a price collapse in 1998, OPEC
members are demanding a "fair" price for their oil. And what they
see as fair is not what consuming nations accept.

Producers are in no mood to do favours for consumer economies
battling against slowdown and recession. Producers were there two
years ago, and consumers not only failed to mourn, but scarcely
even noticed. Revenue—and the battle over oil's economic rent—
have once again taken centre stage. And an emboldened OPEC
is pressing home its advantage (see pp. 8–11).

Revival
As with most revivals, not everything is as it was. Key OPEC producers Saudi Arabia, Iran and Kuwait are gradually opening up
to foreign investment—rather than wresting control of their oil
industries from the majors as they did 30 years ago. But the same
argument that underlined nationalisation then is driving OPEC's
$25/bl oil policy now.

OPEC members, including Saudi Arabia, believe the industrialised world is denying it justice in the oil markets. In the 'seventies, the majors prevented producing nations from receiving a
fair income for their national treasure. Now it is the greed of high-
tax consumer governments that is attracting OPEC's ire.

The language reflects the trauma OPEC producers suffered following the 1998 price collapse. Those events dominate OPEC thinking, and have fundamentally changed the attitude of even moderate members. Anti-tax rhetoric from OPEC is hardly new. But the organisation has rarely been more united, allowing it to make its position felt.

An increasingly hawkish Saudi Arabia is finding common cause with Venezuela's Hugo Chavez—a populist, self-styled champion of the Third World in true 'seventies fashion. That axis is giving OPEC the solidarity that evaded it for much of the 'nineties. Output discipline has kept markets tight and prices high—turning the screw on consumer governments. When European consumers rebelled last year against fuel taxes, OPEC scented blood. "People always talk about revenues of OPEC. They never talk about [oil tax] revenues of industrialised countries," says Algerian oil minister and OPEC president Chakib Khelil. "Before [consumer governments] point a finger at OPEC, they should probably reduce taxes in their own country."

OPEC's more strident position would not be possible without the consent of Saudi Arabia. It suffered heavily in 1998, and fears a repeat price collapse as global economies slow. Saudi-U.S. relations—crucial to OPEC policy since the United States became a net importer of oil in the early 'seventies—are under strain. U.S. support for a bellicose Israel is acutely embarrassing for the kingdom.

OPEC is not about to wield the oil weapon, 'seventies style. But Saudi Arabia cannot afford to draw accusations that it is doing the United States a favour by pressing for oil price moderation. Although the new administration of George Bush would seem to be the dream team for its Middle East allies, so far Bush has conspicuously failed to demonstrate any special magic in his relations with them. The Saudis certainly did the United States no favours at the OPEC meeting.

When it comes to the impact of energy prices on economic growth, OPEC is at best non-committal, and at worst seemingly in denial. "Oil is not that important to economic growth," said OPEC president Chakib Khelil last week. Riyadh agrees. "We think $25/bl is a fair price," says Saudi oil minister Ali Naimi.

The concept of a fair price is hard to pin down. But there is such a thing as a sustainable price. It is, of necessity, a compromise between buyers and sellers. The difficulty for OPEC's core Mideast Gulf producers is that $25/bl is needed to sustain the unreconstructed state-driven economies of the Middle East. But the experience of the 'seventies shows that high prices eventually unleash a wave of investment in non-OPEC oil and a massive improvement in energy efficiency. This is not what OPEC wants, but what it might get.

OTHER REPORTS OF INDEPENDENT TASK FORCES
SPONSORED BY THE COUNCIL ON FOREIGN RELATIONS

*† *State Department Reform* (2001)
Frank C. Carlucci, Chair; Ian J. Brzezinski, Project Coordinator; Cosponsored with the Center for Strategic and International Studies

† *A Letter to the President and a Memorandum on U.S. Policy Toward Brazil* (2001)
Stephen Robert, Chair; Kenneth Maxwell, Project Director

*† *U.S.-Cuban Relations in the 21st Century: A Follow-on Report* (2001)
Bernard W. Aronson and William D. Rogers, Co-Chairs; Julia Sweig and Walter Russell Mead, Project Directors

† *Toward Greater Peace and Security in Colombia* (2000)
Bob Graham and Brent Scowcroft, Co-Chairs; Michael Shifter, Project Director; Cosponsored with the Inter-American Dialogue

† *Future Directions for U.S. Economic Policy Toward Japan* (2000)
Laura D'Andrea Tyson, Chair; M. Diana Helweg Newton, Project Director

*† *Promoting Sustainable Economies in the Balkans* (2000)
Steven Rattner, Chair; W. Montague Winfield, Project Director

*† *Nonlethal Technologies: Progress and Prospects* (1999)
Richard L. Garwin, Chair; W. Montague Winfield, Project Director

*† *U.S. Policy Toward North Korea: Next Steps* (1999)
Morton I. Abramowitz and James T. Laney, Co-Chairs; Michael J. Green, Project Director

† *Safegarding Prosperity in a Global System: The Future International Financial Architecture* (1999)
Carla A. Hills and Peter G. Peterson, Co-Chairs; Morris Goldstein, Project Director

*† *Strengthening Palestinian Public Institutions* (1999)
Michael Rocard, Chair; Henry Siegman, Project Director

*† *U.S. Policy Toward Northeastern Europe* (1999)
Zbigniew Brzezinski, Chair; F. Stephen Larrabee, Project Director

*† *The Future of Transatlantic Relations* (1999)
Robert D. Blackwill, Chair and Project Director

*† *U.S.-Cuban Relations in the 21st Century* (1999)
Bernard W. Aronson and William D. Rogers, Co-Chairs; Walter Russell Mead, Project Director

*† *After the Tests: U.S. Policy Toward India and Pakistan* (1998)
Richard N. Haas and Morton H. Halperin, Co-Chairs; Cosponsored by the Brookings Institution

*† *Managing Change on the Korean Peninsula* (1998)
Morton I. Abramowitz and James T. Laney, Co-Chairs; Michael J. Green, Project Director

*† *Promoting U.S. Economic Relations with Africa* (1998)
Peggy Dulany and Frank Savage, Co-Chairs; Salih Booker, Project Director

† *U.S. Middle East Policy and the Peace Process* (1997)
Henry Siegman, Project Director

† *Russia, Its Neighbors, and an Enlarging NATO* (1997)
Richard G. Lugar, Chair; Victoria Nuland, Project Director

*† *Differentiated Containment: U.S. Policy Toward Iran and Iraq* (1997)
Zbigniew Brzezinski and Brent Scowcroft, Co-Chairs; Richard Murphy, Project Director

---

†Available on the Council on Foreign Relations website at www.cfr.org.
*Available from Brookings Institution Press. To order, call 1-800-275-1447.